THE SHOTGUN IN COMBAT

TONY LESCE

Paladin Press
Boulder, Colorado

The Shotgun in Combat
by Tony Lesce
Copyright © 1984 by Paladin Press

ISBN 0-87364-314-3
Printed in the United States of America

Published by Paladin Press, a division of
Paladin Enterprises, Inc., P.O. Box 1307,
Boulder, Colorado 80306, USA.
(303) 443-7250

Direct inquiries and/or orders to the above address.

All rights reserved. Except for use in a review, no
portion of this book may be reproduced in any form
without the express written permission of the publisher.

Neither the author nor the publisher assumes
any responsibility for the use or misuse of
information contained in this book.

TABLE OF CONTENTS

Introduction 1
A Brief History Of The Shotgun 3
Shotgun Ballistics 5
Shotgun Patterning 18
Penetration Of Shotgun Loads 36
Shotgun Wounds 62
Vulnerability Of The Human Body 65
Advantages and Disadvantages Of The Shotgun 74
Basic Combat Use Of The Shotgun 77
A Quick Review Of Basic Tactics 92
Using The Shotgun In Combat 94
Police Use Of The Shotgun 97
The Shotgun For Home Defense 99
A Sample Plan For Home Defense 110
The Conditioned Reflex 115
Preparing For Combat 118
Miscellaneous Situations 126
Selected Shotgun Scenarios 133
Questions & Answers 137

Types Of Shotguns

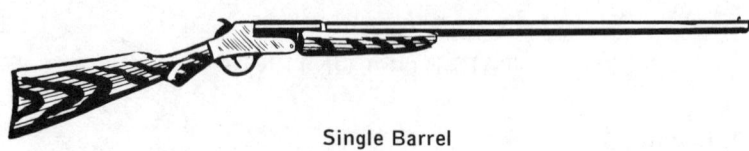

Single Barrel

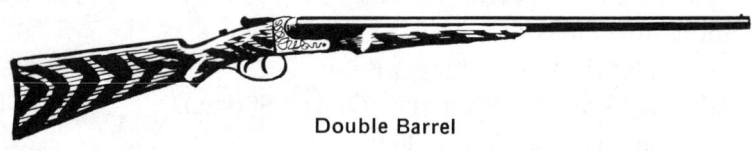

Double Barrel

Pump or Slide Action

Autoloading

Introduction

In the mystique and folklore of "combat" shooting, the pistol is supreme. Most of the fiction and the texts emphasize the use of the pistol and all but ignore the shotgun and the rifle. In competitive shooting, "combat" matches are mainly pistol matches, with an occasional concession to the carbine or the shotgun. The pistol has a mystique, an aura of glamor, that the long arms lack. The pistol and its use have been romanticized beyond all reason by fiction writers and even some non-fiction writers so that it occupies a position out of proportion to its importance and effectiveness.

The shotgun is a workhorse. Although some of the expensive hunting shotguns have the graceful lines of a rifle, most of them, including the short and stubby "riot guns" do not. Some of them are sawn off, for concealment, and this does not add to their looks. Shotguns are made for firepower, not beauty. While arguments rage over the alleged "stopping power" of various pistol cartridges, no one doubts that the shotgun is an effective birth certificate cancellation machine.

The shotgun is easier to learn to shoot. It is deadly. Despite this, little recognition is given it. In the notorious shootout at the O.K. Corral, it has been lost to history how many of the opposing faction were dispatched by "Doc" Holliday's ten gauge sawed off. In the popularizations that ensued, the place of honor was given to Wyatt Earp and his six-shooter. There was even a TV series about his adventures. There was none about "Doc" Holliday and his deadly shotgun.

One of the most violent motion pictures of the last decade, "Dirty Harry," stars a .44 magnum revolver. Perhaps as a result of that picture, the price of a Smith and Wesson Model 29, the gun used in the movie, has gone out of sight. Today a first-quality combat shotgun can be bought for less than half the price of a Model 29.

Recently some of the more realistic police and crime movies and television shows have begun to show the shotgun in a limited way. For example, "Police Story" and "The New Centurions" show the shotgun used by police in certain high-

THE SHOTGUN IN COMBAT

risk situations, such as stakeouts, bank robbery calls, and civil disturbances. "The Godfather" showed the shotgun being used by criminals. Still, accuracy is sacrificed for the story line in most cases. The shotgun is usually shown as an offensive weapon, rather than defensive, and its effects are exaggerated. In one instance, a felon shotgunned by a policeman is shown being picked up bodily by the blast and hurled through a plate glass window. The homeowner armed with a shotgun is neglected. The shotgun in other applications is replaced in fiction by the submachine gun, which makes a more impressive noise.

This text will deal in facts, not fiction. The rationale of the shotgun will be explained, its characteristics and use laid out. We will delve into types of shotguns, their advantages and disadvantages. We will go into the ballistics and their application to practical situations. We will deal comprehensively with the tactics of the shotgun, and how the presence of a shotgun can affect a shootout in relation to other arms. We will not neglect the many modifications and innovations that have been made to adapt shotguns to various needs.

You will see that the shotgun is an arm that offers many advantages and few disadvantages. It is an arm that will give you a great margin of superiority in a firefight, if properly used. It is a simple and practical weapon, a good thing to have along when you go to war.

A Brief History Of The Shotgun

If you define a shotgun as a firearm with an unrifled barrel, then the first firearm was a shotgun and the only type of firearm in existence for centuries was the shotgun.

The date of the first firearm is hazy. Various authorities place the date sometime in the thirteenth or fourteenth century. The ones that fired multiple projectiles are comparable to what is usually thought of as a shotgun, while the ones that fired a ball can be thought of as firing a slug. The early ones were all run on black powder and had various types of delicate and vulnerable ignition systems, such as the matchlock, wheelock, and flintlock.

Rifling came into limited use in the middle of the sixteenth century, thereby establishing a clear-cut distinction between rifles and shotguns. The military, however, did not universally adopt rifling until the end of the eighteenth century and the beginning of the nineteenth. The reason seems to have been a combination of expense, maintenance, and the fact that there were not very many soldiers proficient enough to make full use of the enhanced accuracy provided by rifling the bore. In the American revolution, for example, most of the arms used by both sides were of the category called "smoothbore muskets." Essentially, they fired slugs. The slugs were round lead balls. A few elite units were armed with rifles and did show the military commands what could be done with more accurate and long-ranged arms.

By the middle of the nineteenth century the distinction was clear-cut and universally recognized. Henceforth, the development of rifles and shotguns proceeded in two different directions. The development of the metallic cartridge paved the way for the magazine rifle. The magazine shotgun lagged a bit but by the turn of the twentieth century was in large scale production, although many old-timers still put their faith in the old double barrel shotgun.

The shotgun was widely employed in the development of the American West, much more than most writing and drama dealing with the era acknowledge. Many settler families used

THE SHOTGUN IN COMBAT

the shotgun as the workaday weapon, with the rifle as second favorite. The pistol was expensive and short-ranged and very limited in usefulness. Few, in fact, owned one.

The Spencer and Winchester repeating shotguns made their appearance in the 1880's. The Spencer was the first of the pump or trombone action shotguns, having the cartridges in a tube under the barrel. This is a type which is still in use today, while the Winchester design, with a lever operated action, is almost forgotten.

Farmers and ranchers who had to defend themselves often did so with a shotgun. The expression "riding shotgun" refers to the armament of the guard on stagecoaches. Often, in the struggle between lawmen and outlaws the shotgun played a major part. The shootout at the O.K. Corral is an illustration of this, although there is controversy to this day as to who were the outlaws and who were the lawmen.

With the coming of the present century the military once more used shotguns but this time as a separate and distinct arm. The pump action type seems to be the favorite of the army, and has been made by Winchester, Remington, and Ithaca for the U.S. Army. In the First World War, the advantages in the jungle and in fighting in close quarters assured the shotgun of a role with the armed forces. Folding shotguns are used in Air Force survival kits.

The police use shotguns loaded with buckshot or slugs. Many civilians use them for hunting but also for home defense. In many states with strict gun control laws they are the only weapon that is both practical and available for this purpose.

The shotgun has developed over the years but it has in many ways stayed simple and practical. In the future, its usefulness will increase, not decrease.

Shotgun Ballistics

It is apparent from even a superficial examination of the ballistic figures and the practical destructive effects that the shotgun is more effective and deadly than the pistol. Indeed, its effectiveness is comparable to that of most high power rifles, at short ranges. Even a novice can infer this from the shotgun's heavy recoil. Any weapon that pushes out approximately an ounce of lead at upwards of a thousand feet per second will have a significant kick.

The shotgun is mainly a short range weapon. With a rifled slug the maximum range is about one hundred yards. With No. 00 buckshot the maximum is in the fifty yard bracket. With smaller shot you can count on a smaller effective range. Compared with a hundred yard range for a typical centerfire pistol, with some magnums being considered competent out to two and three hundred yards, the shotgun does not seem impressive. Against a rifle its range seems grossly inadequate.

A Brief table of shot weights and ballistics follows:

TYPE	WEIGHT grains	DIA. inches	VELOCITY F. P. S.	MUZZLE ENERGY
No. 4 buck	20.5	.240	1300	77
00 buck	54	.330	1325	211
12 ga. slug	400	.680	1300	1500
16 ga. slug	350	.630	1300	1313
20 ga. slug	280	.580	1300	1050

A short discussion of the above is essential. First, the validity of the figures. They are mostly taken from standard and authoritative reference works except for the weights, which were taken from cutting apart shotshells and actually weighing the projectiles. Velocities are averaged from several sources and are approximations. It is impossible to be very precise about velocities because they are affected by variables such as barrel length and bore, manufacturing tolerances, and the brand of the ammunition, to name a few. The muzzle energy figures are mathematically derived from weight and

THE SHOTGUN IN COMBAT

velocity and subject to the same variations. Moreover, the figures given for buckshot apply for one pellet only. For No. 4 buck, there are twenty seven pellets in the shell. Therefore the energy of the whole charge is 27x77 FT/LBS., or 2079 FT/LBS. For No. 00 buck, there are nine pellets to the charge. 211x9 gives 1899. The paper figures can be misleading, however. You might think that on the basis of muzzle energy the No. 4 buckshot load will be the most powerful one. This is true, but only at the muzzle. Because the No. 4 pellet is the smallest and lightest of the ones listed, its speed will decay fastest.

It should be noted that the heavier a projectile is, the better ballistic coefficient it has, and the further it will carry. An example of this is the No. 00 buck pellet, which starts out with a muzzle energy of 211 foot-pounds and retains, at fifty yards, only 136 foot-pounds. The No. 4 loses even more. That is quite a drop, unlike many rifle and pistol loadings and unlike the rifled slug. What this means in plain language is that the lighter your projectile the less your killing or disabling range is.

The basic formula for calculating the effective range of your shotgun is this: Multiply the pellet energy by the number of pellets you expect to hit the target at a given range. This gives you the total kinetic energy on target, not allowing for loss of velocity through air resistance. Multiply your magic figure of fifty-eight foot-pounds several times to allow for this factor. Your kinetic energy delivered on target should, in other words, be several times larger than your magic figure.

Where does this magic figure of fifty-eight foot-pounds come from? It is the classical figure used by the U.S. Army as the standard for measuring a disabling hit. Not only has this traditional figure stood the test of time but recently it has been confirmed by the U.S. Army's studies of wounding power of missiles.

How does it relate to "stopping power," a concept used by some gun writers to compare various calibers of weapons for effectiveness? Well, not much. Whether you accept the concept of "stopping power" or not, when you calculate

THE SHOTGUN IN COMBAT

figures for such a powerful projectile as a rifled slug, it's a whole new ball game. When you consider buckshot, you have the factor of multiple hits, and this is far deadlier than a single hit. The army's study suggested that multiple hits are deadlier than single ones in proportion to the square of their number. This should be obvious when you consider that even 2000 ft/lbs in a single missile hit destroys only one area, while if this kinetic energy is distributed over ten different impact points, you have ten different areas being destroyed or disrupted, ten chances instead of one of hitting a vital area, ten times the shock and bleeding, even though each one receives only 200 ft/lbs. This is what makes the No. 4 buck load such a killer at ranges up to about fifty feet, before its velocity falls off very much.

From the above you can see that the 12 gauge is the big daddy of the commonly available gauges. Some are not listed, for example, the 28 gauge and the .410, because they are not quite in the same class. This is not to say that they are not deadly if properly used. They are most certainly not toys but they don't have enough of the devastating punch that characterizes what we have come to think of as a shotgun.

Police and military forces use the 12 gauge. There are larger gauges available on special order but the 12 is the largest commonly available one.

There are some Magnum loads available for the shotgun, for example a twelve-pellet No. 00 load that is terrifying to fire. It is one-third more powerful than the standard load but the increased recoil and blast are not worth it. The nine pellets of the standard load are more than good enough.

How many of your pellets will hit your target at a given range? The only way to tell for your shotgun is to do some patterning tests, as illustrated in some of the photographs in this book. The size of your pattern will vary with your barrel length, degree of choke if any, load, and brand of ammunition. Manufacturers' figures are only an approximation. Often they're good enough, but if you want to be precise run your own tests.

THE SHOTGUN IN COMBAT

ADDITIONAL NOTES ON AMMUNITION AND ACCESSORIES

SILENCERS

To my knowledge, silencers in conjunction with a shotgun have never before been discussed in print. Part of the reason is that a silencer would add to the weight and bulk of an already large weapon. Another reason is that silencers are illegal, unless you get a special dispensation from the Federal Government.

With all that, it is still possible to say something about them. First, it would be superfluous to have a silencer in most situations in which a shotgun would be useful. You just don't need one.

Second, a silencer for a shotgun is large and difficult to make. A twelve-gauge shotgun has a large charge and generates a large volume of hot gas compared to a pistol or a rifle. To contain such a volume of gas and dissipate its energy without an explosive noise is possible only if you pay no attention to bulk and weight of the device.

It would be extremely foolish to admit in print to having tested or owned a silencer, much less having manufactured one.

DUTCH LOADS

As pointed out in "Shoot-out," Dutch loads are a mix of ammunition loaded into the magazine of your weapon. They are needed because situations are unpredictable and very changeable. For example, if you are a police officer assigned to stakeout duty in a store, you might choose to put a couple of No. 4 Buck loads in the magazine so that they feed first. This takes care of the initial stage of the action, in which you are likely to be facing the felons close-up. They may, instead of giving up, choose to run for it. If you don't put them down with the first couple of blasts you will want something more substantial in the chamber as the range opens up. You might choose No. 00 Buck. If the felons make it to the

THE SHOTGUN IN COMBAT

getaway car or are behind a barricade, you would welcome the longer range and increased penetrating power of a slug. Therefore, if you have a pump gun with a seven shot tubular magazine you might choose to insert three slugs first, then two of No. 00, and finally a couple of No. 4's. The chamber would be empty to start and the first shells to come under the hammer would be the small shot.

If, on the other hand, you are involved in an ambush, you may choose to reverse the order, loading the slugs last on the supposition that your target will be in a car which you must first penetrate and disable, hence the slugs. For close-in work and mopping up you will want buckshot.

If you are carrying a shotgun routinely and cannot predict the situation which you will face you probably would want to alternate slugs and shot in the tube. That way you'd be at worst one shell away from the needed load.

POISONED LOADS

This subject was treated extensively in "Shoot-out," along with the rationale for using poisoned bullets. For shotguns, they are even easier to make but less necessary, as the shotgun is a deadlier weapon and your target is more likely to succumb to the wound before the poison acts. Nevertheless, some targets are hit with only the edge of the pattern (assuming that you are firing shot and not slugs) and it would be helpful if some noxious substances were introduced into his bloodstream at the same time.

Because of the large size of a shotshell a large amount of poison can be mixed in with the shot. This can be done while loading or, if you do not load your own, opening up factory ammo and inserting it into the compartment that holds the shot.

It is not necessary to have unusually toxic substances when you load them into a shotshell. The large amount you can fire makes up for any inadequacy in the poison. Even rat poison will do. It should be in crystalline form so that it will fire along with the charge and be carried to the target or it should be a thick liquid that will coat the individual pellets.

THE SHOTGUN IN COMBAT

TESTING YOUR AMMO FOR RELIABILITY

With a shotgun, as with any other weapon, you need trouble-free operation if you are to survive a gunfight. It is important to run at least a magazine full of the brand and type of ammunition you contemplate using through the gun to check for trouble free operation. Jacking the shells through the action won't do. It is dangerous if you try this at home, as an accident can always happen, and it does not tell you anything about the ease of extraction of the fired shells. You might find that the fired shells hang up enough to impede smooth operation of the action.

Reliability of ignition is so obvious that it is often overlooked. It does you no good to load super-magnum triple-ought buck if they misfire. This should be checked out just as carefully as you do mechanical operation. It can only be done by firing trials. Jacking the shells through the action will not prove anything, again.

Some shooters are so addicted to the practice of jacking their ammunition through the action that they forget what it does and does not prove. All this practice can establish is that the ammunition is mechanically within tolerance when introduced into the action. It does serve a useful purpose in checking out a new box of an ammunition type that has previously been tested and proven satisfactory.

IMPROVISED LOADS FOR THE SHOTGUN

It is useless to give reloading data for the shotgun here when there are many excellent books on the subject. Some are reloading manuals put out by the powder companies, others are manuals put out by manufacturers of reloading equipment and other components. They all have extensive information on the subject.

The only limitation on reloading for combat use of which we are aware is that rifled slugs and No. 00 buckshot are difficult to obtain. For some reason or other they are not commonly available.

THE SHOTGUN IN COMBAT

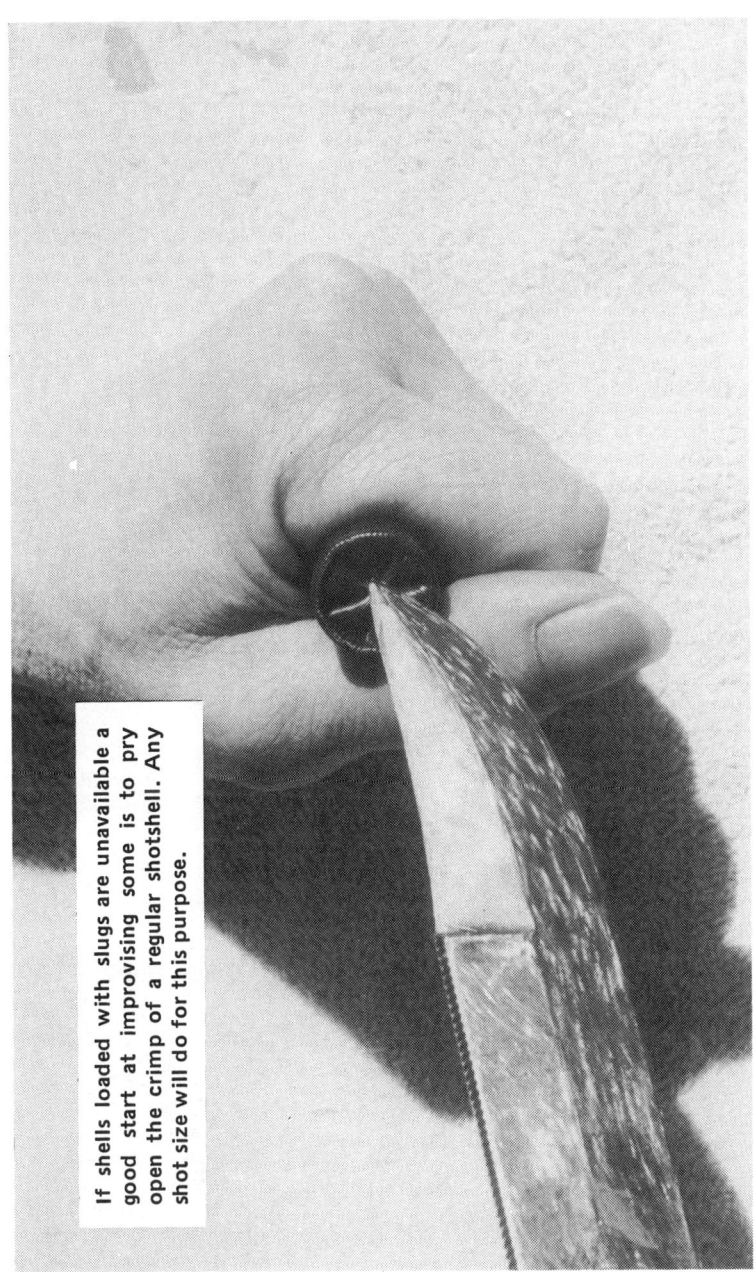

If shells loaded with slugs are unavailable a good start at improvising some is to pry open the crimp of a regular shotshell. Any shot size will do for this purpose.

THE SHOTGUN IN COMBAT

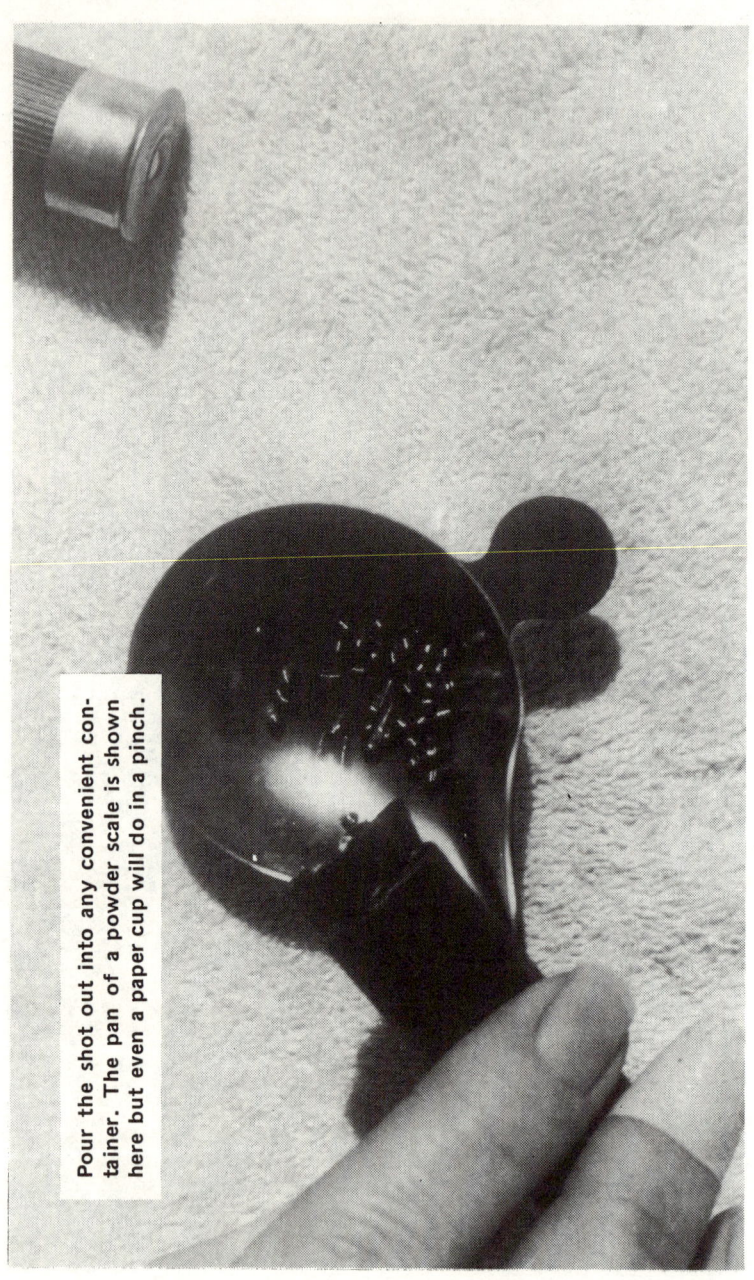

Pour the shot out into any convenient container. The pan of a powder scale is shown here but even a paper cup will do in a pinch.

THE SHOTGUN IN COMBAT

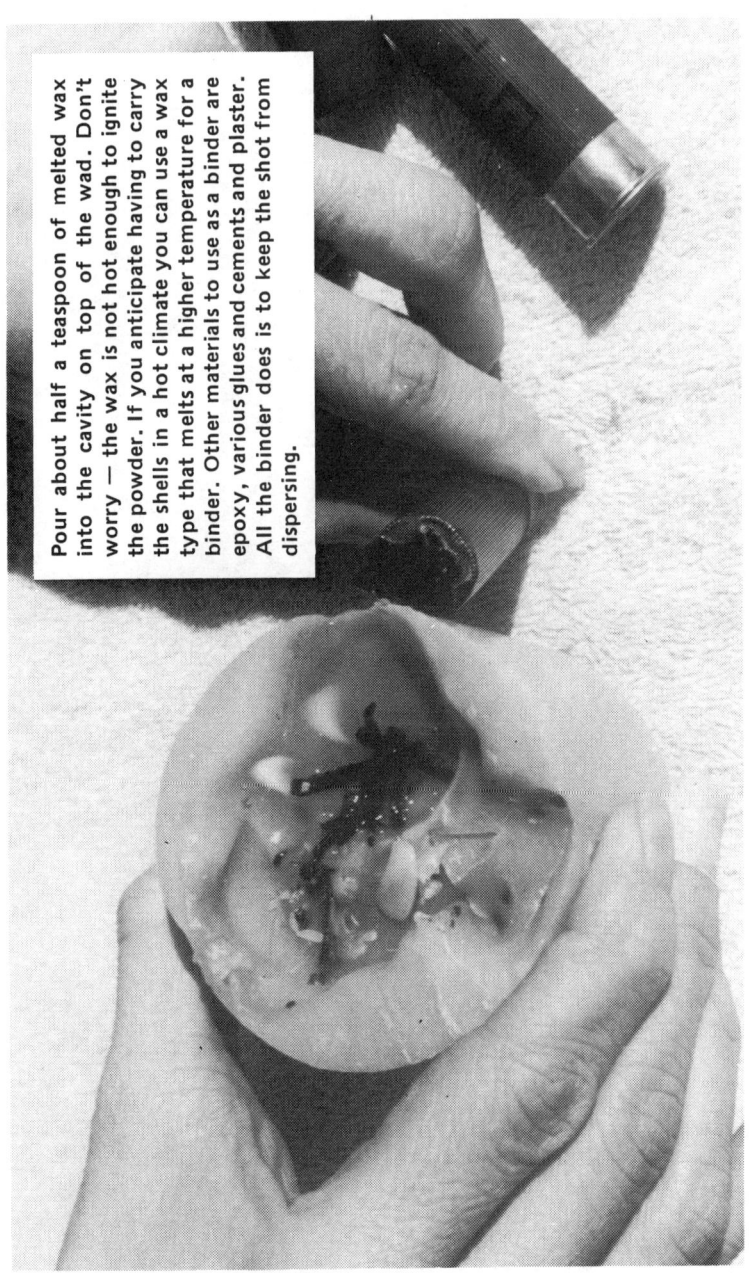

Pour about half a teaspoon of melted wax into the cavity on top of the wad. Don't worry — the wax is not hot enough to ignite the powder. If you anticipate having to carry the shells in a hot climate you can use a wax type that melts at a higher temperature for a binder. Other materials to use as a binder are epoxy, various glues and cements and plaster. All the binder does is to keep the shot from dispersing.

THE SHOTGUN IN COMBAT

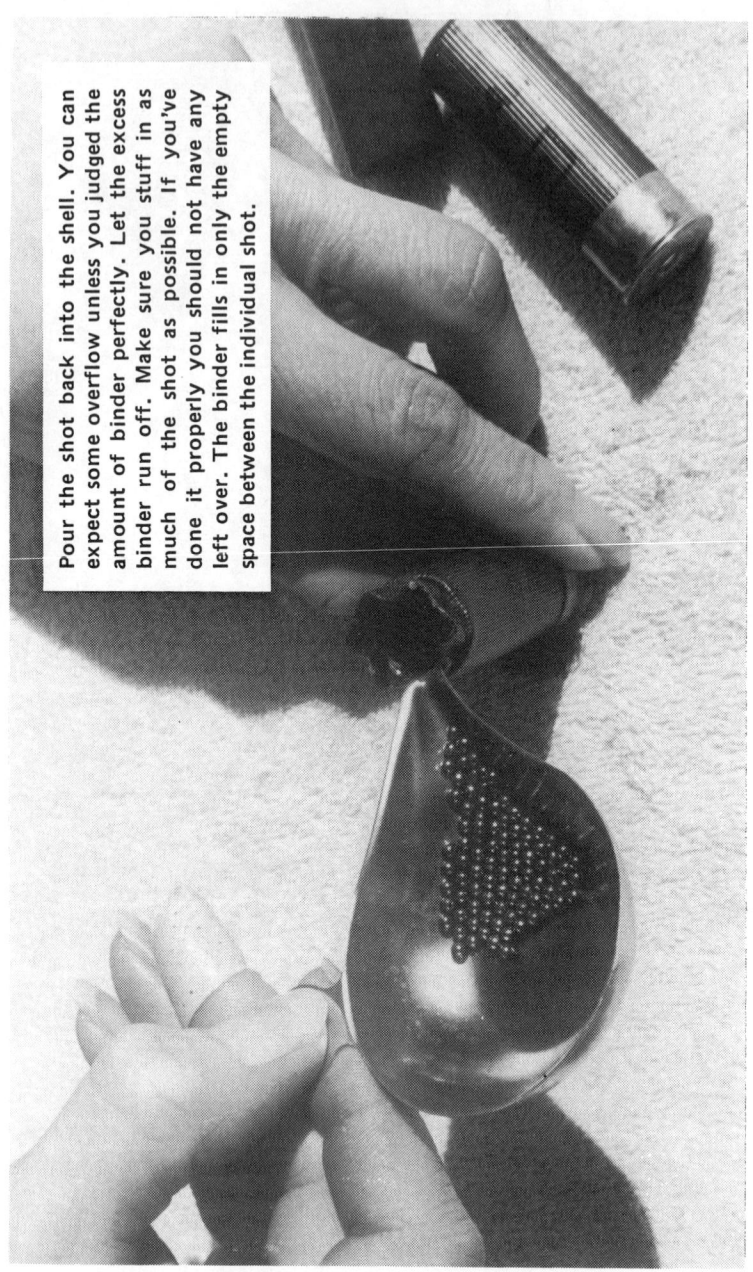

Pour the shot back into the shell. You can expect some overflow unless you judged the amount of binder perfectly. Let the excess binder run off. Make sure you stuff in as much of the shot as possible. If you've done it properly you should not have any left over. The binder fills in only the empty space between the individual shot.

THE SHOTGUN IN COMBAT

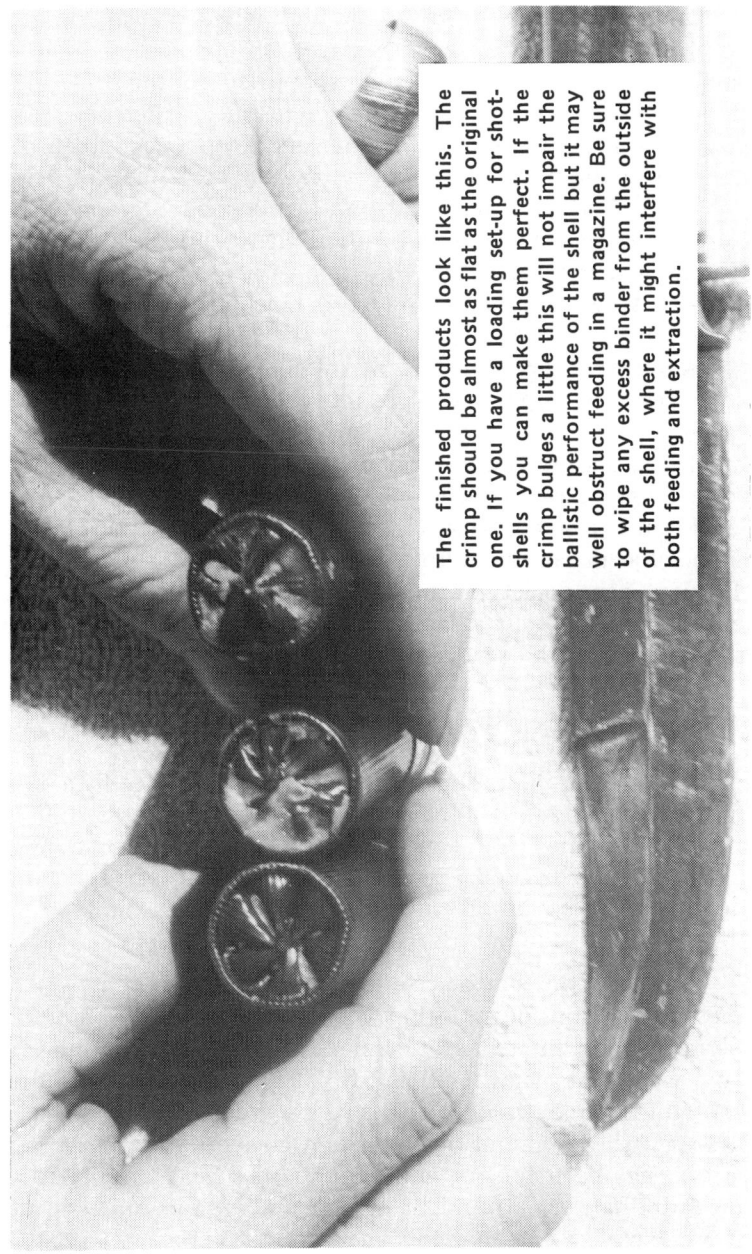

The finished products look like this. The crimp should be almost as flat as the original one. If you have a loading set-up for shotshells you can make them perfect. If the crimp bulges a little this will not impair the ballistic performance of the shell but it may well obstruct feeding in a magazine. Be sure to wipe any excess binder from the outside of the shell, where it might interfere with both feeding and extraction.

THE SHOTGUN IN COMBAT

That points up the need for improvised loads. For example, rifled slugs can by jury-rigged by opening up a shotshell, whatever the size it contains, pouring out the shot, and pouring it back with melted wax as a filler. When the wax cools it will bind the shot together and keep it together as it goes down the barrel and towards the target. We tried it and it works. The accompanying photographs show graphically how it's done. The improvised slugs have everything but the rifling, which means that they are very effective at short ranges. At longer ranges they are more effective than unwaxed shot.

An ultra short range load, suitable for use in built up areas, can be improvised by emptying out a shotshell and refilling it with BB's. If you can get steel shot that size so much the better. The lesser density of steel projectiles makes for a lower ballistic coefficient and a shorter range.

In an extreme case, rock salt, nuts, bolts, screws, or any small objects can make up a short range load for a shotgun. The lesser the density of the projectiles, the shorter the range, but they are equally deadly at ten feet. At that range even the wad can produce a deadly wound.

HIDING A SHOTGUN

With the proliferation of gun laws there may come a day when even shotguns will be registered and/or confiscated. For those determined to keep their arms some form of hiding place may be needed. Because of a shotgun's size, a safe deposit box is out of the question. The sheer bulk of a shotgun and its ammunition complicate the problem.

Burial is the simplest solution for many. If that is the method for you, be sure that you dig a deep enough hole to permit placing some boards at the bottom to form a sump for any water that may leak in. It is important to have the shotgun liberally coated with a preservative oil to protect it against rust. Ammunition requires even more care. One way is to place each box of ammunition in a heat seal bag as a moisture barrier. You might include an envelope of dessicant if you have some, as an additional precaution.

THE SHOTGUN IN COMBAT

If you need ready access to the weapon then some sort o of secret compartment in a well or in your car is the answer. There are several books available on how to do this.

Shotgun Patterning

It is unfortunate that the shotgun has come to be nicknamed the "scattergun" by some people. Because of this sobriquet, some have come to believe that the shotgun will wipe out an array of opponents over a wide arc. Others have the misapprehension that aiming is totally unnecessary and that just pointing the shotgun in the general direction of the target is enough. On the other hand the experiences of hunters and skeet shooters have led to the belief that the shotgun must be aimed almost as carefully as the rifle.

The fact is that combat shooting is different than hunting or skeet shooting. Often the weapon will bear only a superficial resemblance to the hunting shotgun. The ranges are often shorter and the targets are much larger. This points up the need for a reappraisal of the shotgun's capabilities.

We conducted firing trials using both a combat type shotgun and a hunting type weapon. We used various types of loads at ranges of ten to ninety feet. The photographs that follow illustrate the patterning that you may expect at various ranges and consist of a photographic superimposition of the pattern upon a human outline. The patterns are to scale, assuming that the silhouette is that of an adult male six feet tall.

Several conclusions are obvious from studying the pictures. First, although it is not necessary to aim the shotgun with pinpoint precision there is not enough scatter, particularly at short ranges, to permit much carelessness. As a corollary, you cannot hope to put down two opponents with the same pattern at ranges under ninety feet unless they are standing shoulder to shoulder.

Second, the effect of a choke on the patterning of the shot is very pronounced. This can be both good and bad. It means that more of your pattern will be on the target at long ranges but also that you have to be even more careful in aiming the shotgun. More hits mean more wounding power. A tighter pattern means less margin for error.

THE SHOTGUN IN COMBAT

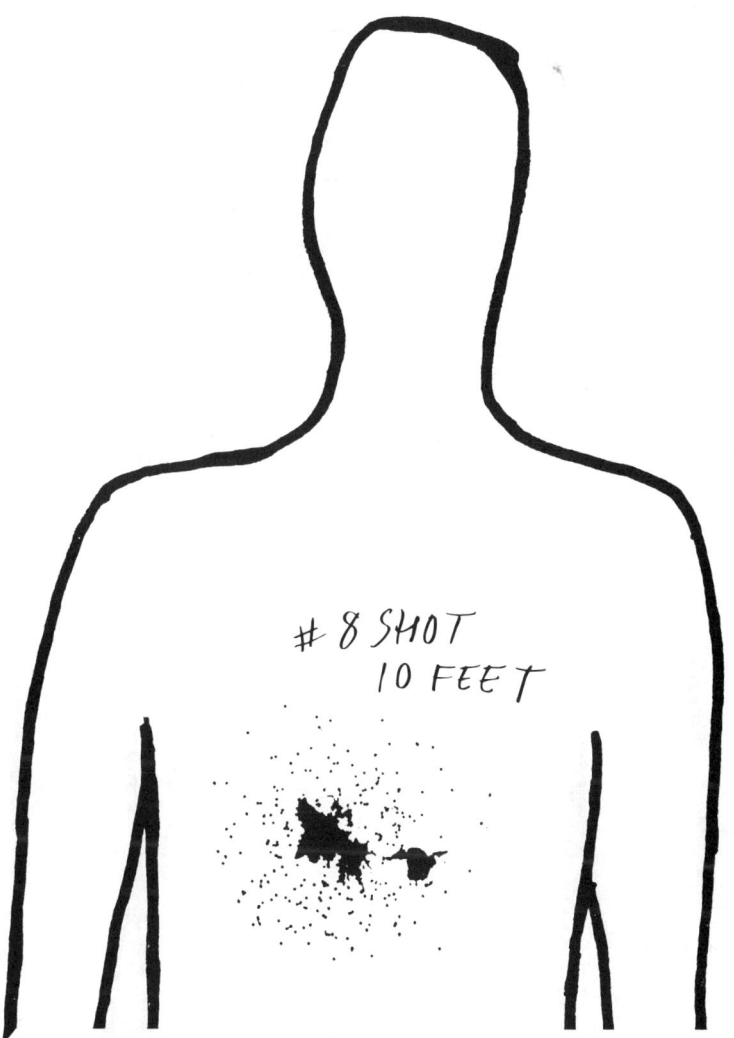

Number 8 bird shot at range of ten feet. Fired from a cylindrical bore shotgun (a sawed-off Mossberg 500 with a barrel length of nineteen inches) at ten feet, the concentrated pattern rips, tears, and shreds its way through the human figure. This illustrates that even a mild hunting load can be very effective in a home defense situation. The main pattern of the charge is on the left of the figure and the ragged hole made by the wad is on the right. There is enough scattering so that if this were a head shot the face and eyes would be severely damaged as well as the back of the head blown out.

THE SHOTGUN IN COMBAT

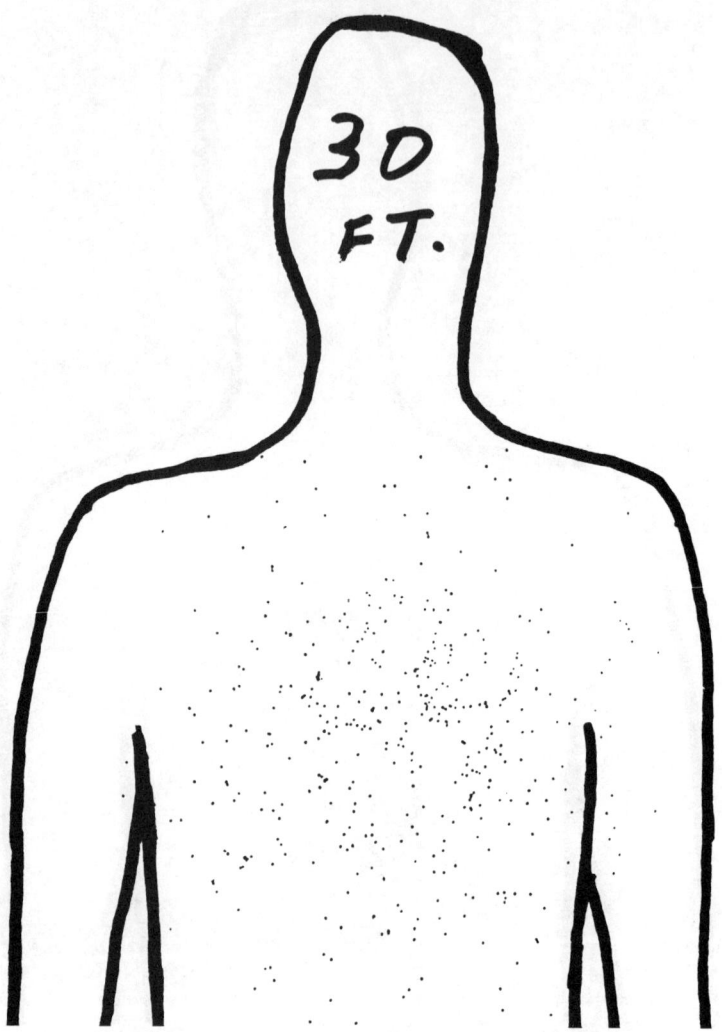

Number 8 bird shot at thirty feet range. Again fired from a cylindrical bore shotgun, this pattern shows enough dispersion to cover the entire torso. There is no concentration of shot to punch its way through the ribs and make the nasty, tearing wound that so often results in an immediate fatality. On the other hand, an opponent hit in the face with this one would be immediately disabled and perhaps blinded for life. Locating this pattern a little higher would result in damage to the unprotected neck area, containing the windpipe and the blood vessels supplying the brain with blood. This would be a lethal injury.

THE SHOTGUN IN COMBAT

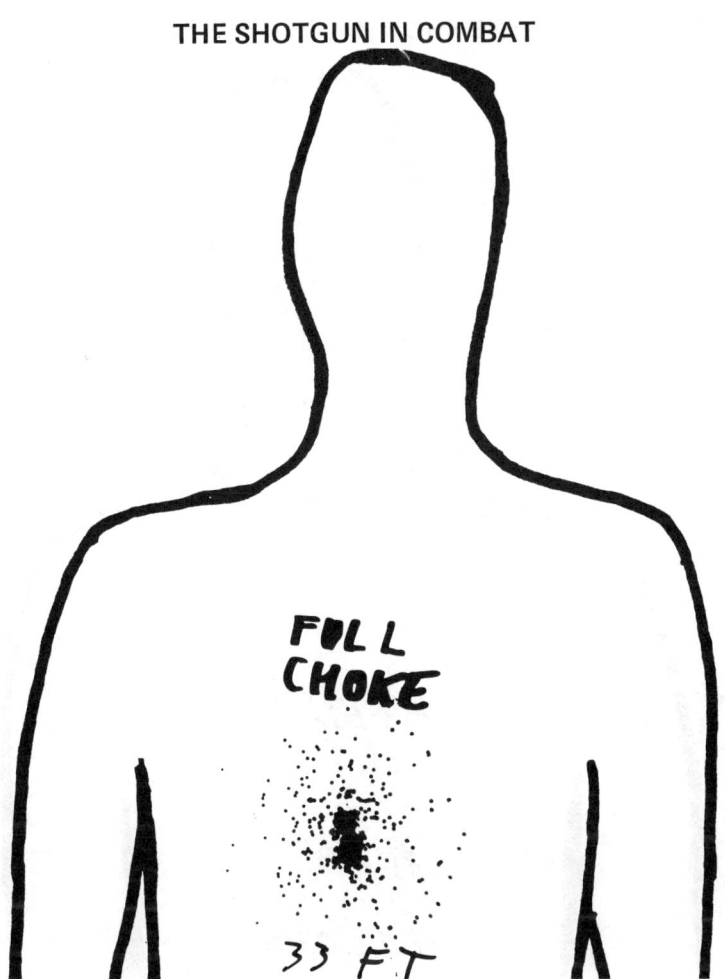

Number 8 bird shot showing the effect of full choke. This pattern, fired at the same range as that in the previous picture, shows a pattern almost as tight as that fired at ten feet. Again, there is that punching effect that breaks ribs and penetrates to vital organs. In this case the heart, lungs, and central blood vessels would be involved, assuring an immediate fatality. The gun involved is a Harrington & Richardson "Topper," a simple and light gun in the very bottom price bracket. It is "only" a single shot weapon but producing a wound such as this obviates the need for a second shot. This type of weapon is more likely to be found in the home than the police-type pump repeater. The magazine gun is better for handling multiple opponents but with the judicious use of cover and some dextrous reloading the defender using the single shot is not in a hopeless position.

THE SHOTGUN IN COMBAT

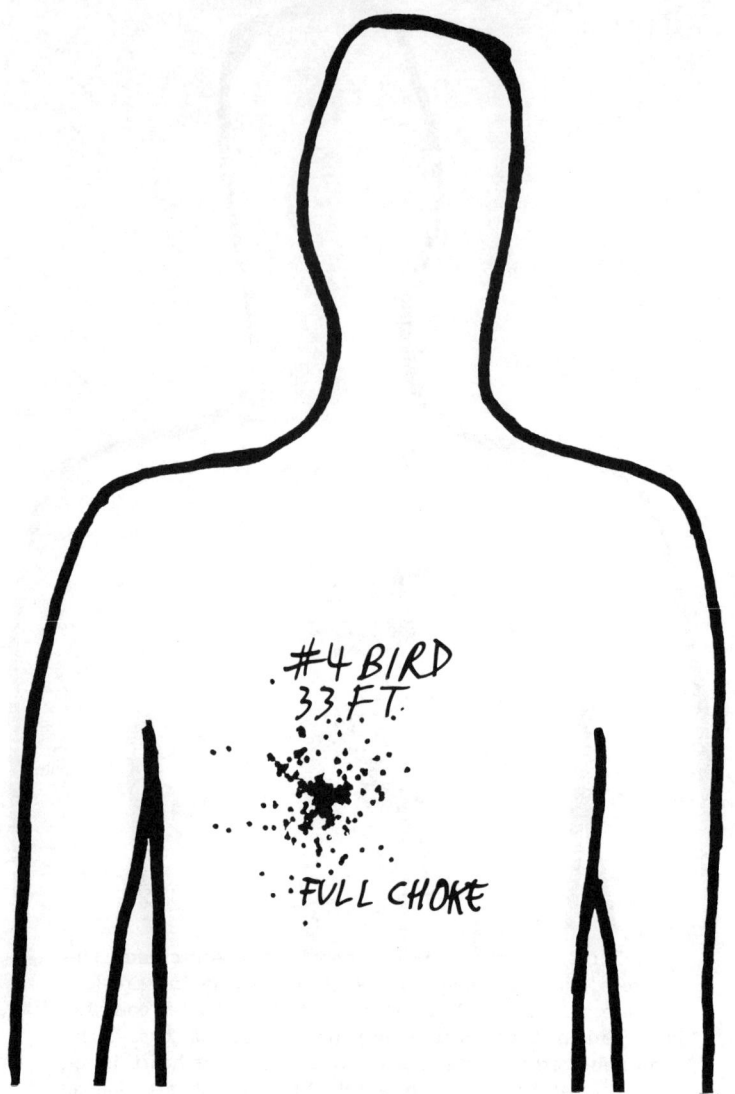

Number 4 bird shot at thirty-three feet, full choke. There are fewer pellets but this shows the same concentrated pattern that looked so lethal in the previous photo. Because the pellets are larger, they have more sectional density and better carrying power than the number 8 shot. They would be effective out to a longer range.

THE SHOTGUN IN COMBAT

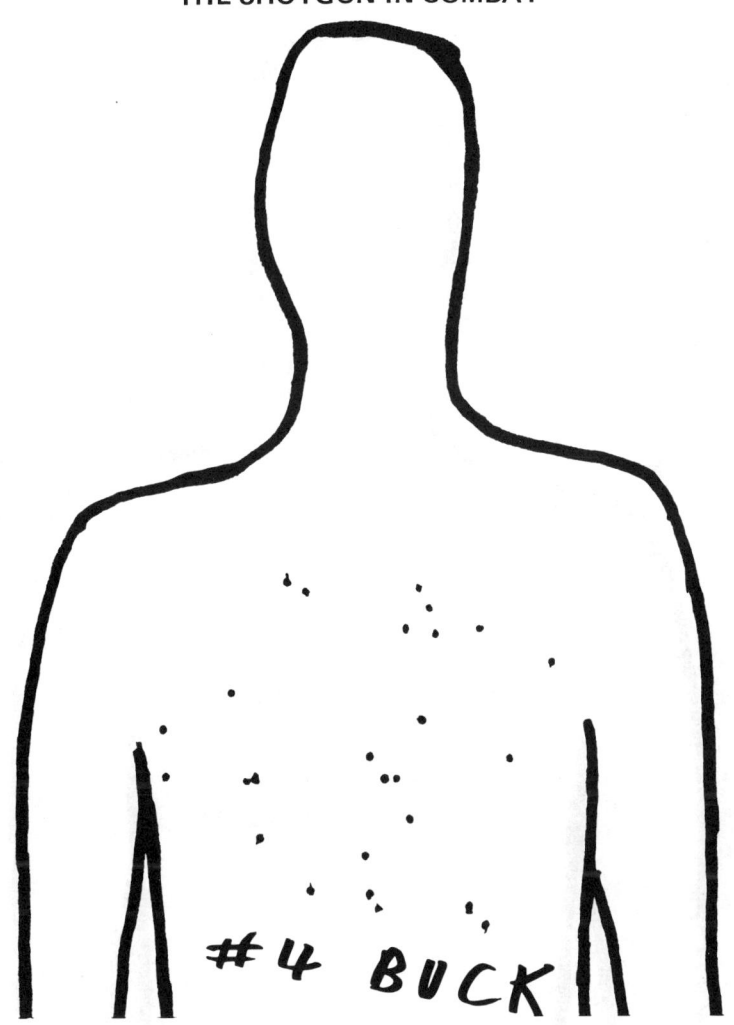

Number 4 buckshot fired at thirty feet, cylindrical bore. Many believe that number four buck is the best all-round load and looking at this pattern it is easy to see why. The twenty seven pellets are evenly scattered on the target. This can be compared to twenty-seven hits with a .24 caliber pistol. The heart, lungs, and various blood vessels would be damaged, making for a surely fatal result. Additionally, Number 4 shot is heavy enough not to be seriously impeded by heavy clothing as would Number 8 shot at this range. In fact, a jacket and heavy overcoat might well make the difference between life and death if the shot is too small.

THE SHOTGUN IN COMBAT

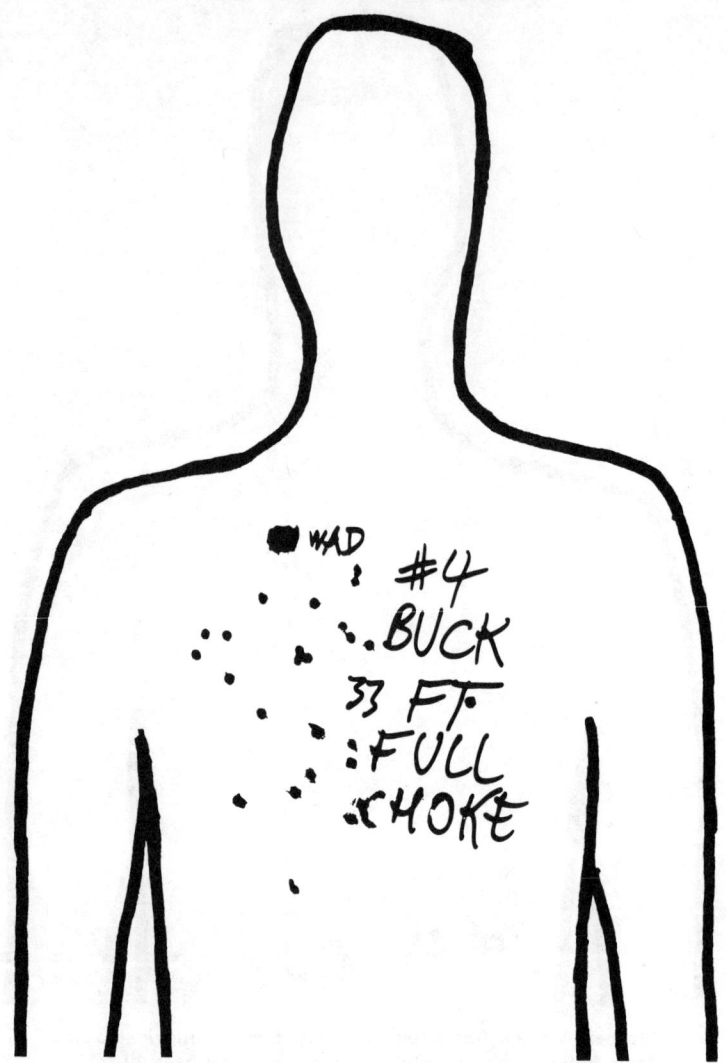

Number 4 buck, thirty-three feet, full choke. Characteristically, the pattern is tighter with the full choke. In this photo the hole made by the wad can be seen, although at this range the wad would probably not have enough force to make a lethal wound. The shot, however, would. The pattern, slightly off center here, would hit both lungs, the heart, and the major blood vessels in the center of the body. A head shot would not only involve the brain and the eyes but would severely lacerate the windpipe and the blood vessels in the neck, again causing a fatal injury.

THE SHOTGUN IN COMBAT

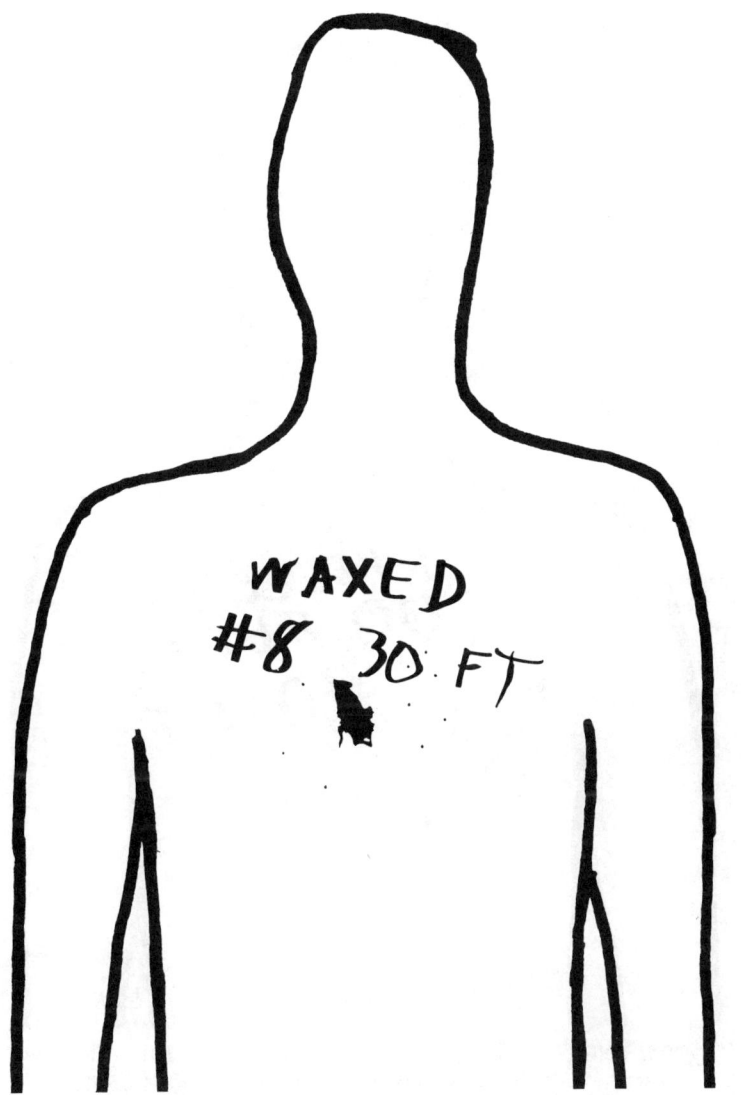

Fired at thirty feet, the improvised slug looks like this. Notice that most of the shot held together — only a dozen or so scattered. They would have held together even better if epoxy instead of wax had been used.

THE SHOTGUN IN COMBAT

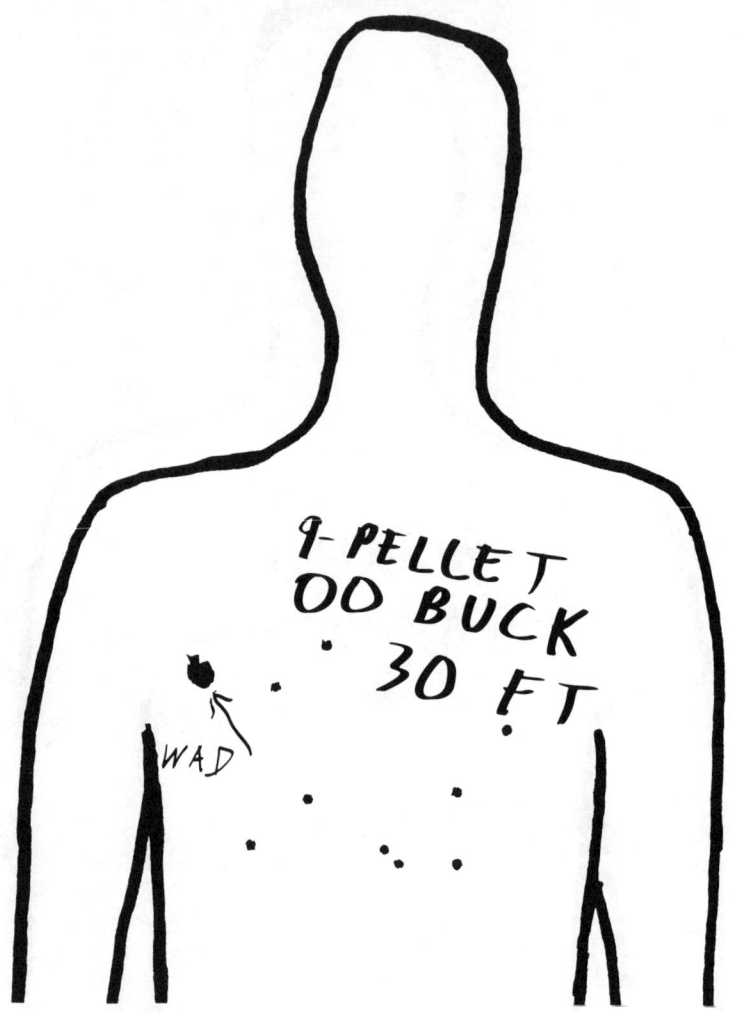

Nine pellet No. 00, cylindrical bore, thirty feet. This is the pattern made by a standard double-ought, the favorite police load. The pellets are scattered enough to involve the heart and lungs, and would surely penetrate any likely clothing worn by the subject. The wad, whose impact can be seen in the upper left, can penetrate paper at this range but not much more. Double-ought is noted for penetrating car bodies, not surprising considering that the pellet is .33 caliber and weighs fifty-four grains.

THE SHOTGUN IN COMBAT

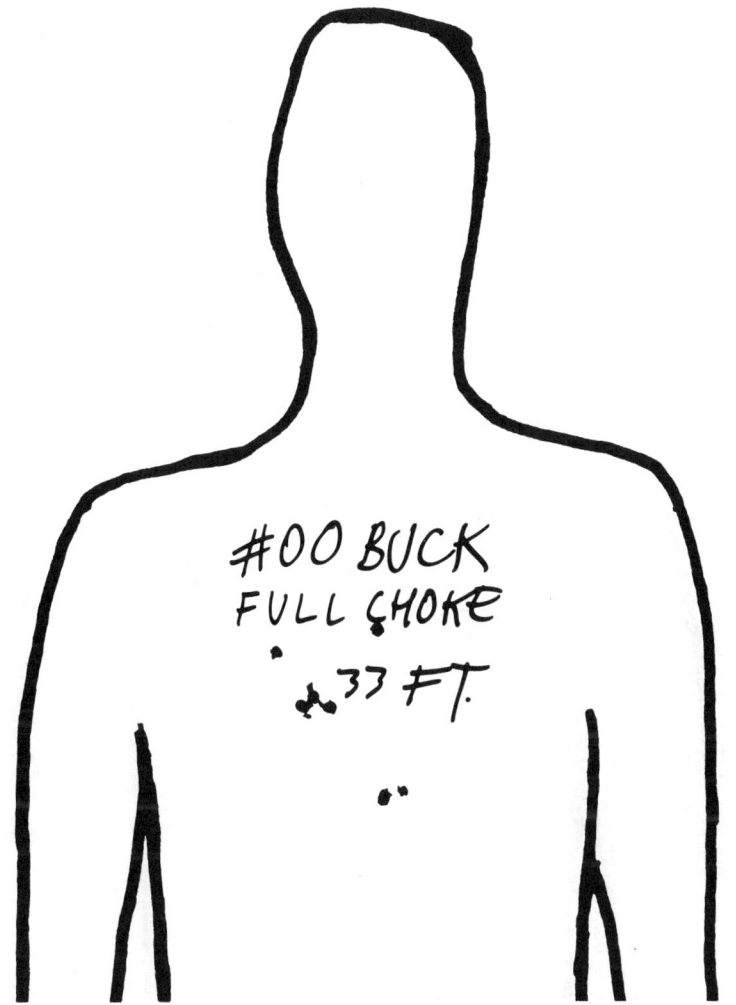

Nine pellet No. 00, full choke at thirty-three feet. The pattern here measures slightly more than half the diameter of that fired from the gun without a choke. The concentrated lethality of the nine pellets striking in area only about six inches in diameter is apparent in this photo. There are only seven holes. Two of them are elongated, suggesting double impacts. These pellets are heavy enough to cause severe damage by breaking off pieces of ribs and thereby generating secondary missiles. Notice that the small diameter of the pattern dictates careful aiming, particularly if all you have is a single shot.

THE SHOTGUN IN COMBAT

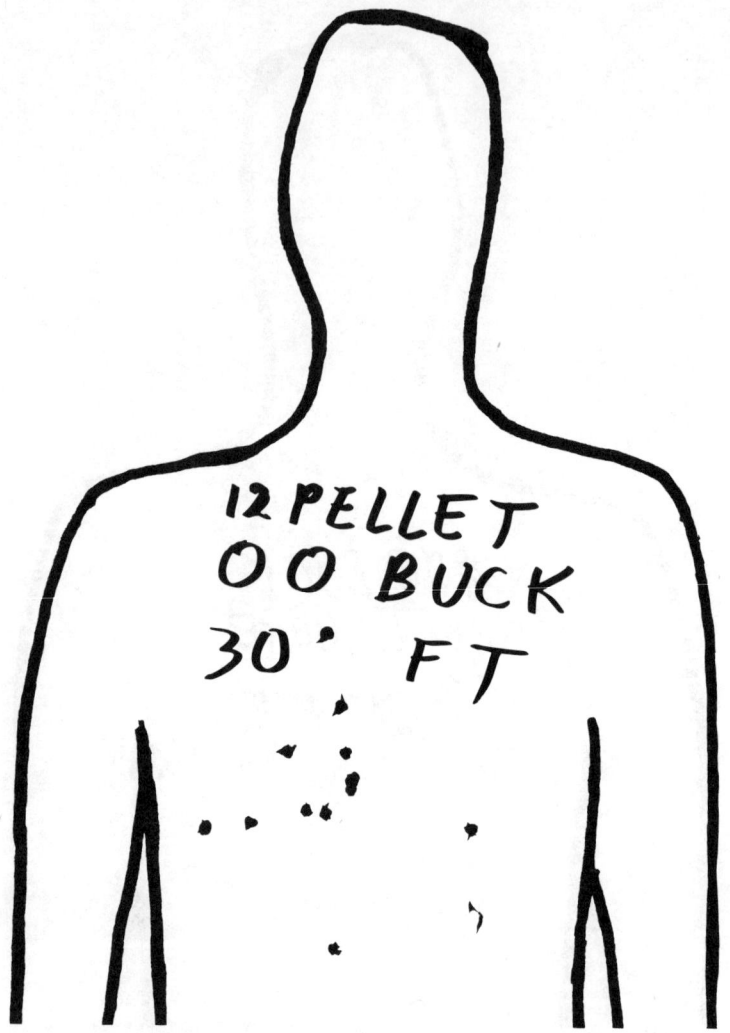

Twelve pellet "Magnum" load, cylindrical bore, thirty feet. The little used "Magnum" load for the twelve gauge has twelve pellets instead of nine, but travels the same velocity. The pattern is about the same diameter as the one made by the regular load, but it is denser, if an increase of three pellets can be labelled as more density. There is one double impact visible in the center of the pattern, right in the region of the heart. The deadliness of the "Magnum" load is beyond question, without implying that the regular load is in any way puny. The increase in recoil is severe, making this load far less popular than the regular one.

THE SHOTGUN IN COMBAT

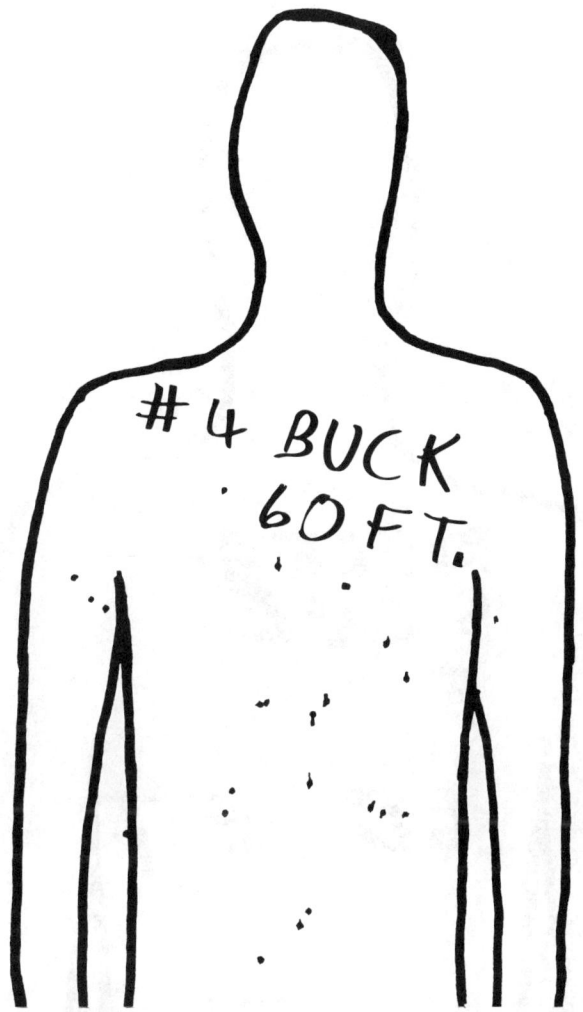

Number 4 buck at sixty feet, cylindrical bore. There are only twenty-three hits visible in this photo, which leads one to assume that the other four went someplace else. The pattern is wide enough to have been capable of engulfing two subjects if they had been standing side by side. The lethality would have been uncertain, however. In this case the hits are evenly distributed between the chest and the abdomen. In the unlikely eventuality that the hits in the heart and lung area did not do the job immediately, the hits in the soft, unprotected abdomen would insure death from peritonitis within a few days, if untreated.

THE SHOTGUN IN COMBAT

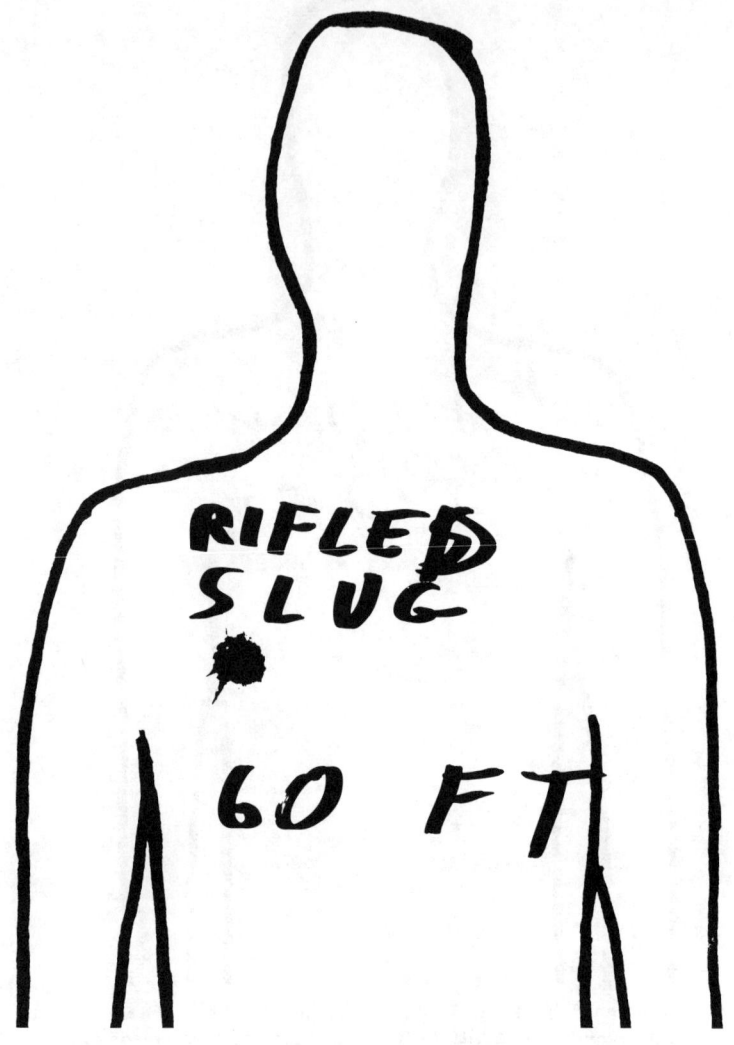

Rifled slug, sixty feet. Four hundred grains of lead travelling at somewhere over a thousand feet per second means impact and wound. In this case the slug would crush ribs and penetrate the lung, causing a severe wound with massive hemorrhage, with additional damage from secondary missiles. Caution: a rifled slug should not be fired from a gun with a choke, as there is danger of overpressure and also damage to the choke.

THE SHOTGUN IN COMBAT

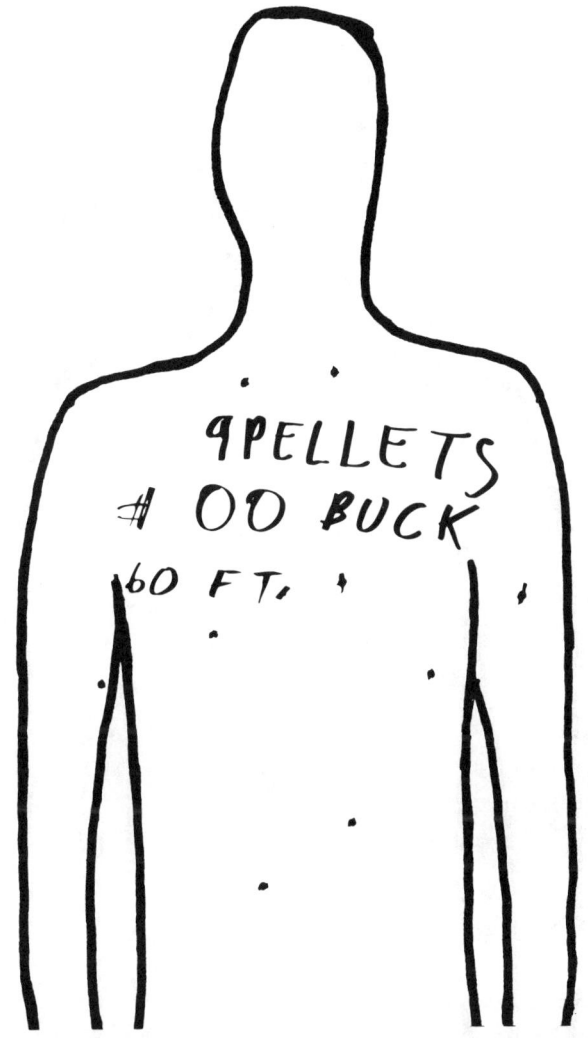

Nine pellets of No. 00, sixty feet, cylindrical bore. In this pattern the hits are well scattered, with two up near the throat, one in each arm, two in the abdominal area and the rest in the chest. Again, the pattern is scattered enough to hit two subjects standing side by side. The effects would be serious, even if the nine pellets were divided between two subjects. As shown, the effect would be a sure fatality, unless a medical miracle were performed, as the tissue destruction would be widespread and severe, hitting several vital areas at the same time.

THE SHOTGUN IN COMBAT

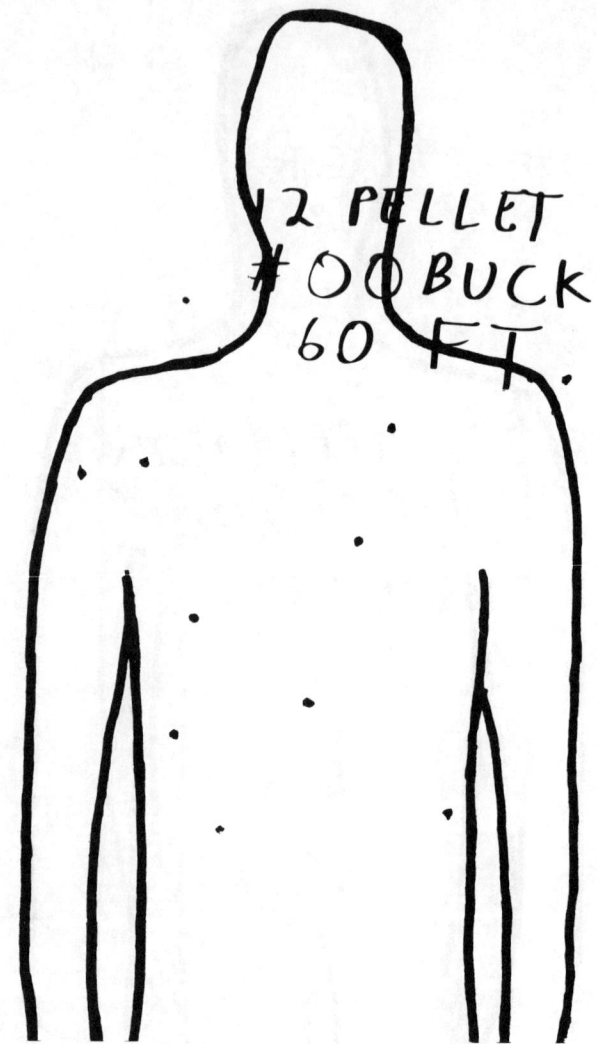

Twelve pellets of No. 00 at sixty feet, cylindrical bore. The scattering effect is such that the "Magnum" load resulted in only nine hits on the subject. Another hit would have been recorded if the aim had been slightly lower. Nevertheless, the nine which did hit caused lethal damage. This load, with more pellets, would have been slightly more effective than the nine pellet load if split between two subjects. Against this is the battering effect of increased recoil.

THE SHOTGUN IN COMBAT

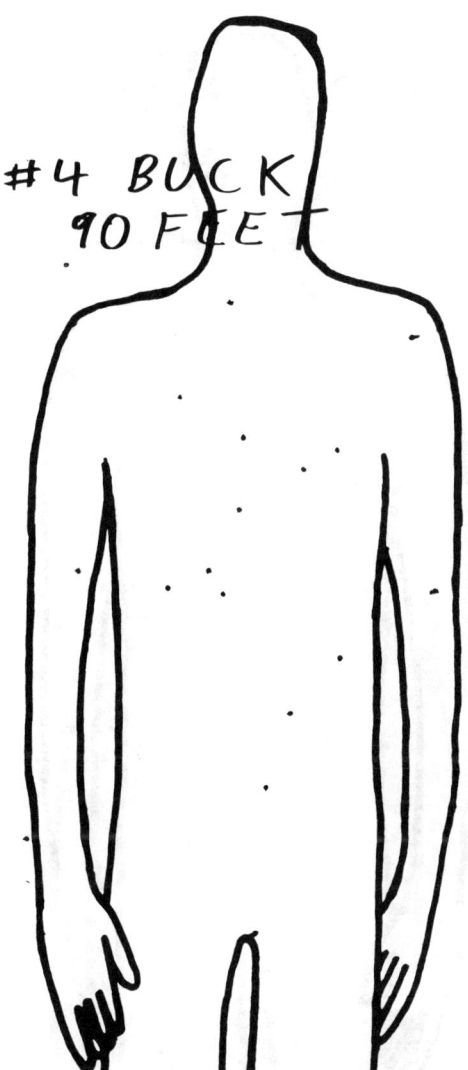

Number 4 buck, ninety feet, cylindrical bore. At ninety feet, the scattering is pronounced, and two subjects standing side by side would have been well peppered. Number four buck is still capable of causing serious injury at this range, even though the velocity of the pellets has fallen off a lot. They may not be able to penetrate the rib cage, depending on the clothing worn by the subject. However, the unprotected areas would still be terribly vulnerable.

THE SHOTGUN IN COMBAT

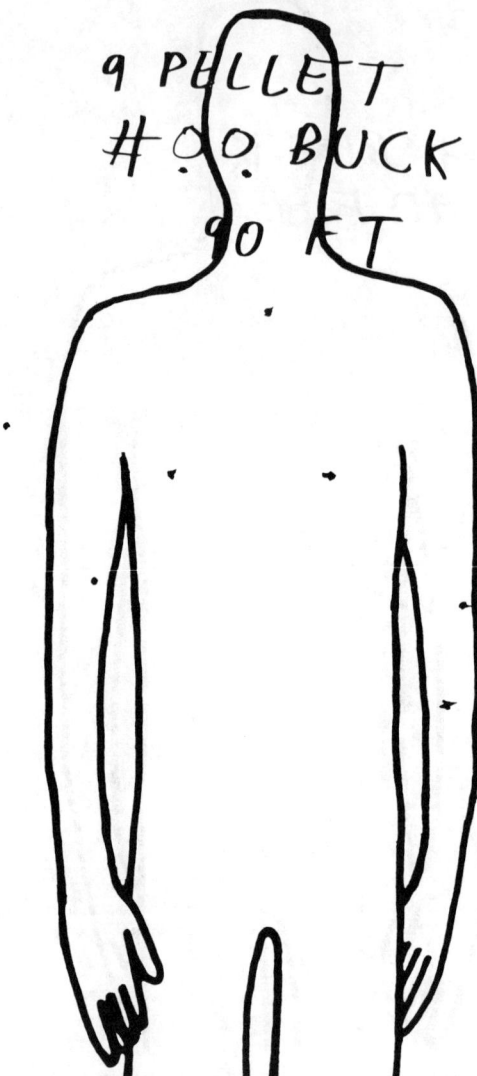

Nine pellets No. 00 buck at ninety feet, cylindrical bore. Seven hits, three of which are in vital areas. This pattern shows a good scattering, enough to hit another subject standing beside the first. A shotgun with a full choke would have concentrated the pattern more for enhanced lethality but a tighter pattern means more careful aiming, as well as precluding taking out two opponents at that range.

THE SHOTGUN IN COMBAT

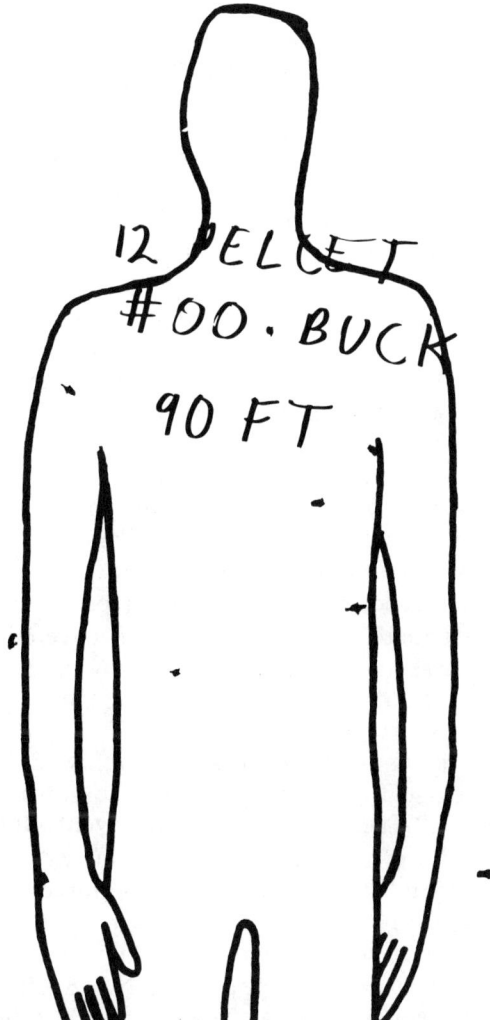

Twelve pellet "Magnum" load, ninety feet, cylindrical bore. Of the twelve pellets, only seven hit the subject and only nine are visible on the paper at all. The twelve pellet load scatters more, making it more suitable for use against multiple opponents. Notice that there is no impact from the wad visible. The wad, being large, light, and of low sectional density, has a very poor ballistic coefficient and does not reach out much beyond thirty feet. Of the seven hits shown here, only two can be said to have hit in vital areas causing immediate serious effects. Nevertheless, seven hits taken together are very serious in their cumulative effect.

Penetration Of Shotgun Loads

One reason why the shotgun is favored by police forces around the country is that it has very limited range and penetration. This is very important in an urban enviroment where it is paramount to avoid injuring or killing innocent people.

It is a truism to say that a shotgun blast is less likely to penetrate a wall and injure innocent people than is a rifle or pistol bullet. There is a scarcity of hard information as to just what sort of wall a weapon will or will not penetrate and at what range. Thus we are left with a few generalizations that are of little help or may be misleading. Because of this we decided to run some firing trials to determine what weapon does what with what load and at what range.

We constructed a section of interior wall as shown in photo No. 1 and took it out to the boonies for our tests. The wall is of standard construction, 2x4's covered with wallboard, and was not reinforced in any way for the tests. There is no insulation and there are no pipes or conduits in the wall.

Our results were somewhat surprising. We did not expect the wall to be so flimsy and permeable to gunfire. All pistol rounds, from .22 through .41 Magnum, went sailing through as if the wall were paper. The exceptions were a .22 and a 9mm that hit studs. They were stopped completely.

All shotgun blasts fired at a range of ten feet went through. It is not surprising that a rifled slug went through but the wall did not even stop some No. 8 birdshot. Even the wads did some damage. The No. 8 shot had enough power left to penetrate a third piece of wallboard placed immediately behind the wall section. This is not, of course, proof of killing power, or stopping power, or anything of the sort, but it clearly indicates that innocent people behind that wall would be injured.

Some of the photos show that the charge hitting a gallon jug of water after passing through the wall still has enough oomph left to blow it up in a spectacular manner. It

THE SHOTGUN IN COMBAT

is obvious that at close range an interior wall is no protection against a shotgun or anything else.

When the range opens up a bit the picture changes somewhat. A charge of No. 8 fired at thirty-three feet penetrated only the near side of the wall section and did not come out the other side. At thirty-three feet, the pattern is scattered enough to offer a good margin if your aim is a little off.

Number four shot is a different story. It is a lot larger and has a better ballistic coefficient, hence, it carries farther. It will penetrate a wall and still have a lot left over. Larger sizes will do even better.

Exterior walls are another story. We tested the impact of various projectiles upon cement blocks and we found that almost nothing does much damage. Pistol bullets of several calibers from .22 up to .41 Magnum just chip the cement blocks. Buckshot roughens the surface. A rifled slug will break the cement block but it will bounce back and not penetrate. We fired at both the unsupported midsection of the cement blocks and the part that was supported by the web. In no case was there a clear case of penetration. We found ricochets in most cases. Of course, it can be safely inferred that a cement block that was supported by a wall of which it formed a part would be somewhat more resistant.

We tested blocks under what we consider to be minimal conditions. In real construction the blocks might be filled with concrete, insulation, or sand. They would be part of a wall. The exterior wall itself might not be constructed of blocks but of bricks or slump blocks, both of which are denser than cement blocks as they are solid throughout. We feel that we can safely conclude that exterior walls constructed of blocks or bricks offer very good protection against gunfire, even the massive impacts of rifled slugs.

Exterior walls constructed of "stucco," which is usually some sort of cement spread over a base made of wallboard and chicken wire, can be expected to have a little more resistance to gunfire than the typical interior wall. This means not very good.

THE SHOTGUN IN COMBAT

The resistance of walls to gunfire can be enhanced very easily and cheaply. Pouring sand into the hollow spaces inside interior walls and cement block exterior walls will double their resistance at the very least. It takes nine inches of sand to stop a .30 caliber rifle bullet. Four inches will stop a .41 Magnum. Three inches of concrete will do it. There are various expedients which can be used to provide protection for yourself and your family in your home.

It is very useful to be aware of the truly minimal protection offered by interior walls. You will perhaps be facing an opponent who takes "cover" behind a wall in the mistaken belief that it is bullet-proof. Knowing that it is not gives you an advantage.

The shotgun is versatile in the sense that it can accept a wide variety of loads. The rifled slug is a good example of one which can make penetration work for you. If you need maximum penetration a slug will penetrate a car body and come out the other side. If there is someone in that car the slug may not make it all the way through. Double-ought will go through one door to wound anyone behind it. Number four is marginal. It depends on the thickness of the metal, whether the window is rolled up or down, and the padding inside the door.

The advantages of using a shotgun in a situation in which a car may be involved are obvious. Not so obvious is the advantage against someone wearing body armor. This is discussed further on in this book.

Section of interior wall built for the firing trials. This was made of standard 2x4 studs covered on both sides with ½" wallboard. There was no insulation on the inside as interior walls are not normally insulated.

THE SHOTGUN IN COMBAT

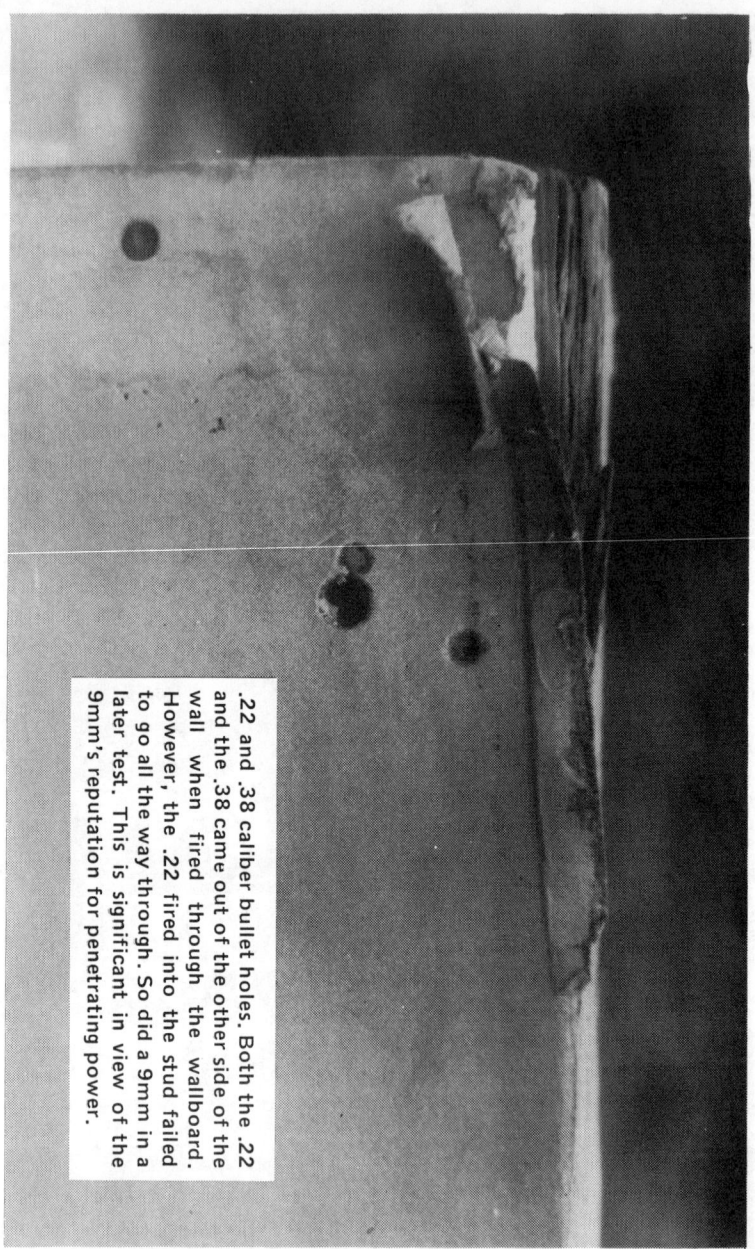

.22 and .38 caliber bullet holes. Both the .22 and the .38 came out of the other side of the wall when fired through the wallboard. However, the .22 fired into the stud failed to go all the way through. So did a 9mm in a later test. This is significant in view of the 9mm's reputation for penetrating power.

THE SHOTGUN IN COMBAT

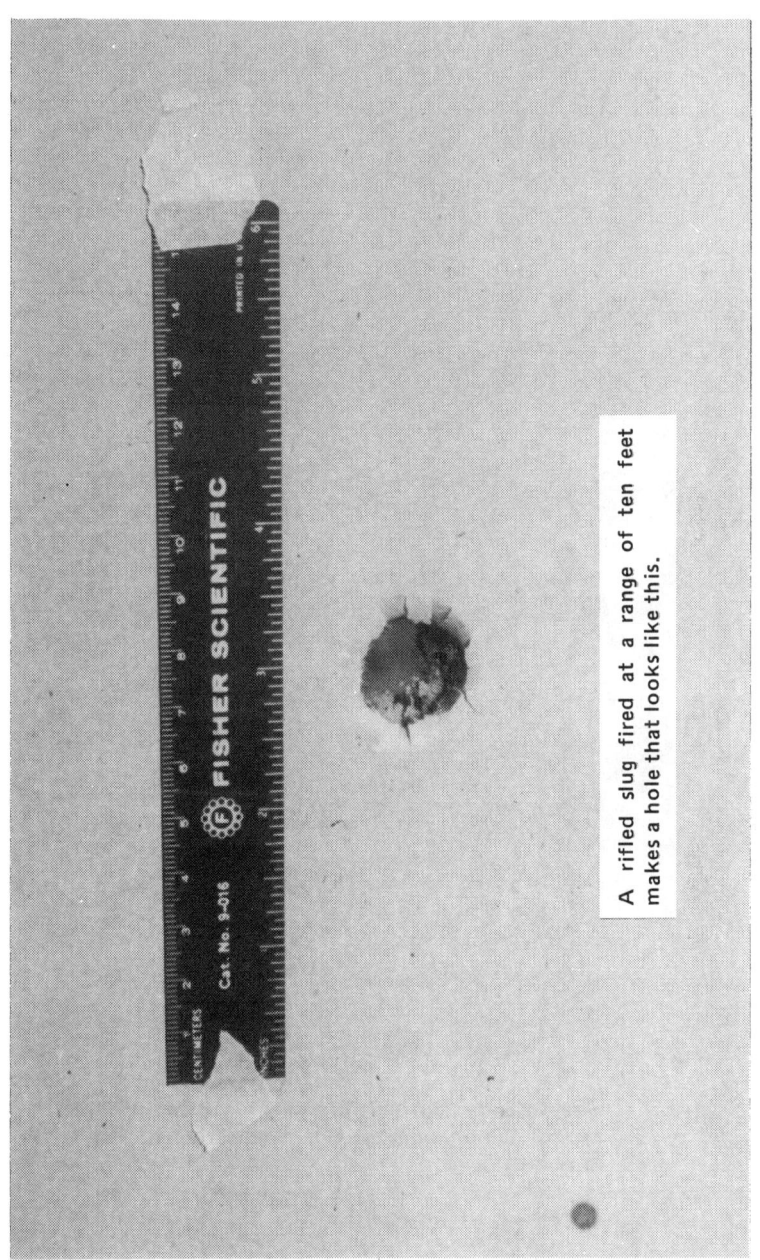

A rifled slug fired at a range of ten feet makes a hole that looks like this.

THE SHOTGUN IN COMBAT

When it comes out the other side it explodes a gallon jug of water, giving an indication of its residual power.

THE SHOTGUN IN COMBAT

The twelve pellets of a magnum charge of No. 00 buckshot, fired at a range of ten feet, sail through the wall section and blow up the water jug behind it. Anyone taking cover behind this wall would be in bad shape.

THE SHOTGUN IN COMBAT

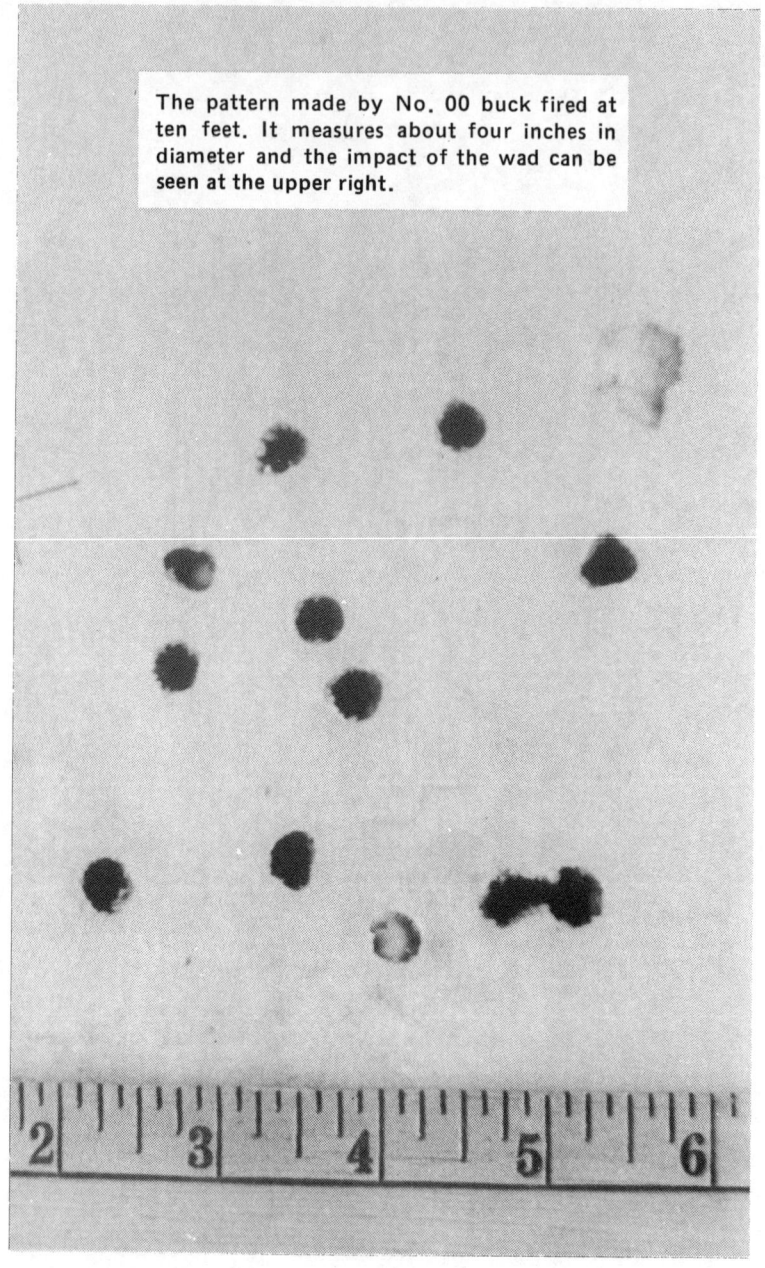

The pattern made by No. 00 buck fired at ten feet. It measures about four inches in diameter and the impact of the wad can be seen at the upper right.

THE SHOTGUN IN COMBAT

Coming out of the other side of the wall, the twelve pellets still retain a lot of their energy after making these frightful looking holes.

THE SHOTGUN IN COMBAT

A charge of twenty seven pellets of No. 4 buckshot blows up a gallon jug after going through the wall.

THE SHOTGUN IN COMBAT

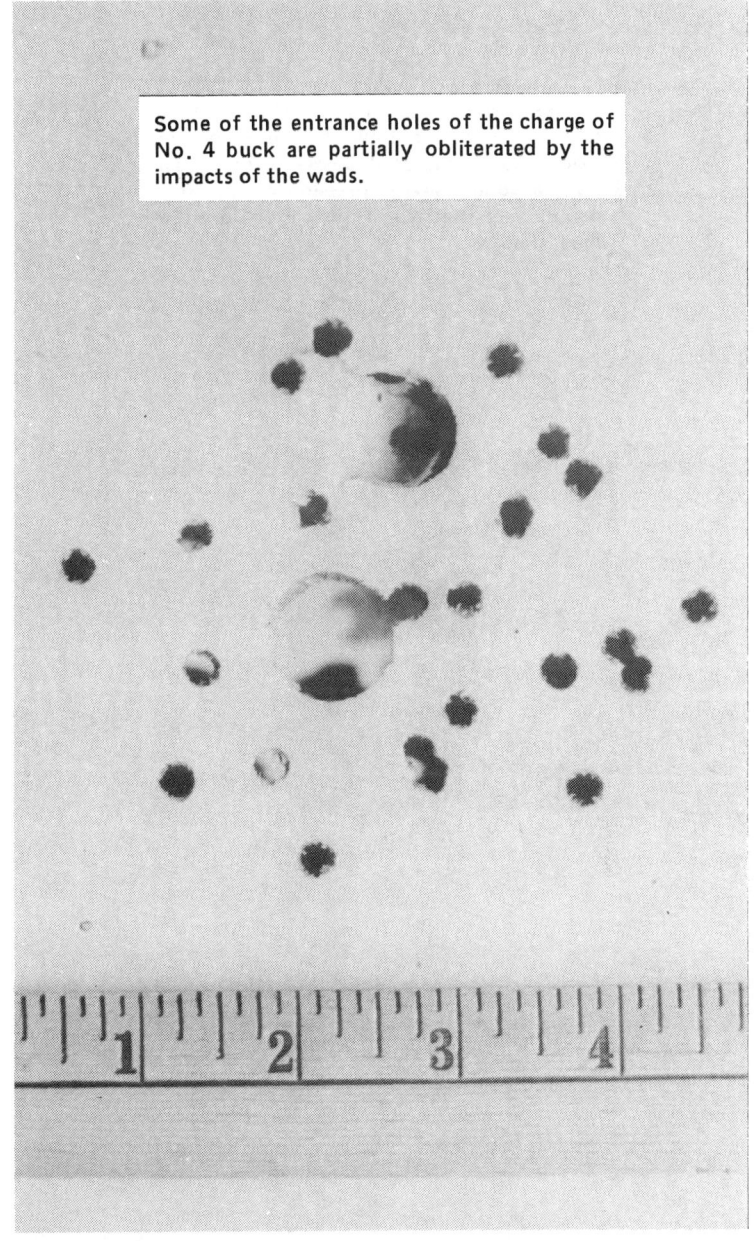

Some of the entrance holes of the charge of No. 4 buck are partially obliterated by the impacts of the wads.

THE SHOTGUN IN COMBAT

The exit holes of the charge of No. 4 blend together, showing how the buckshot rips, tears, and shreds as it passes through. This gives a good visual impression of why some people feel that No. 4 buck is the deadliest load of all.

THE SHOTGUN IN COMBAT

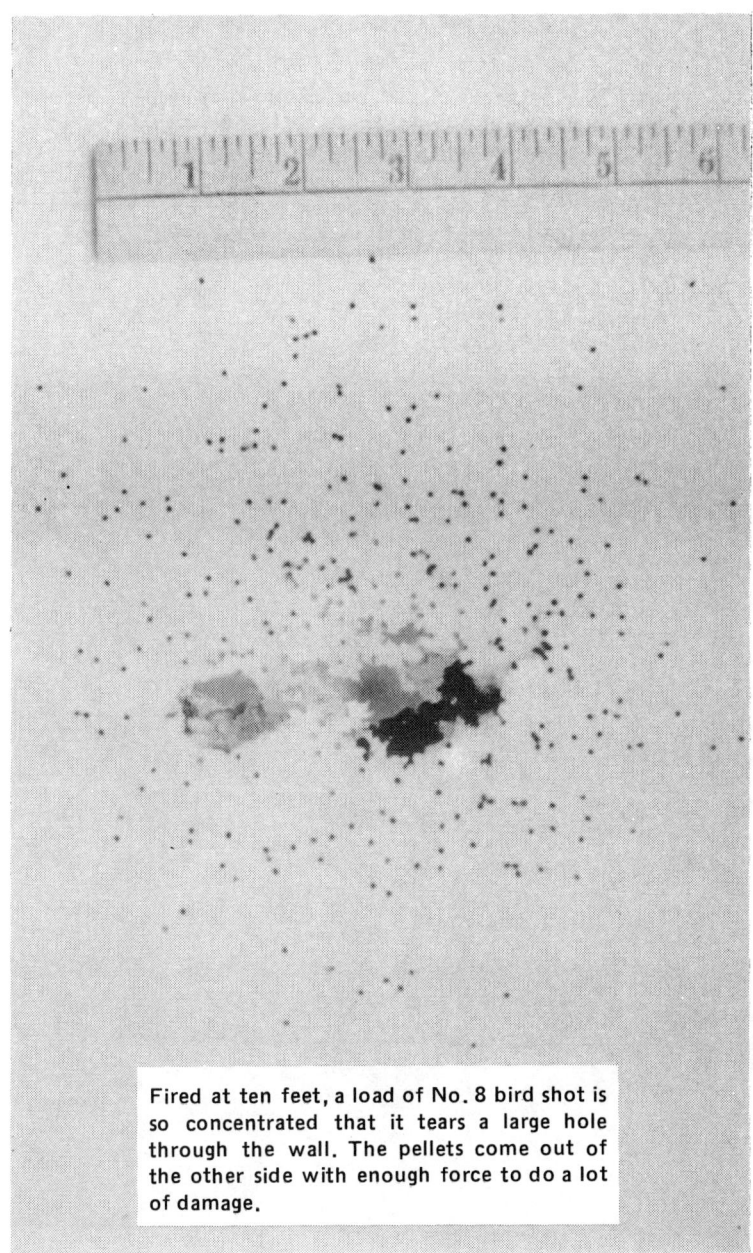

Fired at ten feet, a load of No. 8 bird shot is so concentrated that it tears a large hole through the wall. The pellets come out of the other side with enough force to do a lot of damage.

THE SHOTGUN IN COMBAT

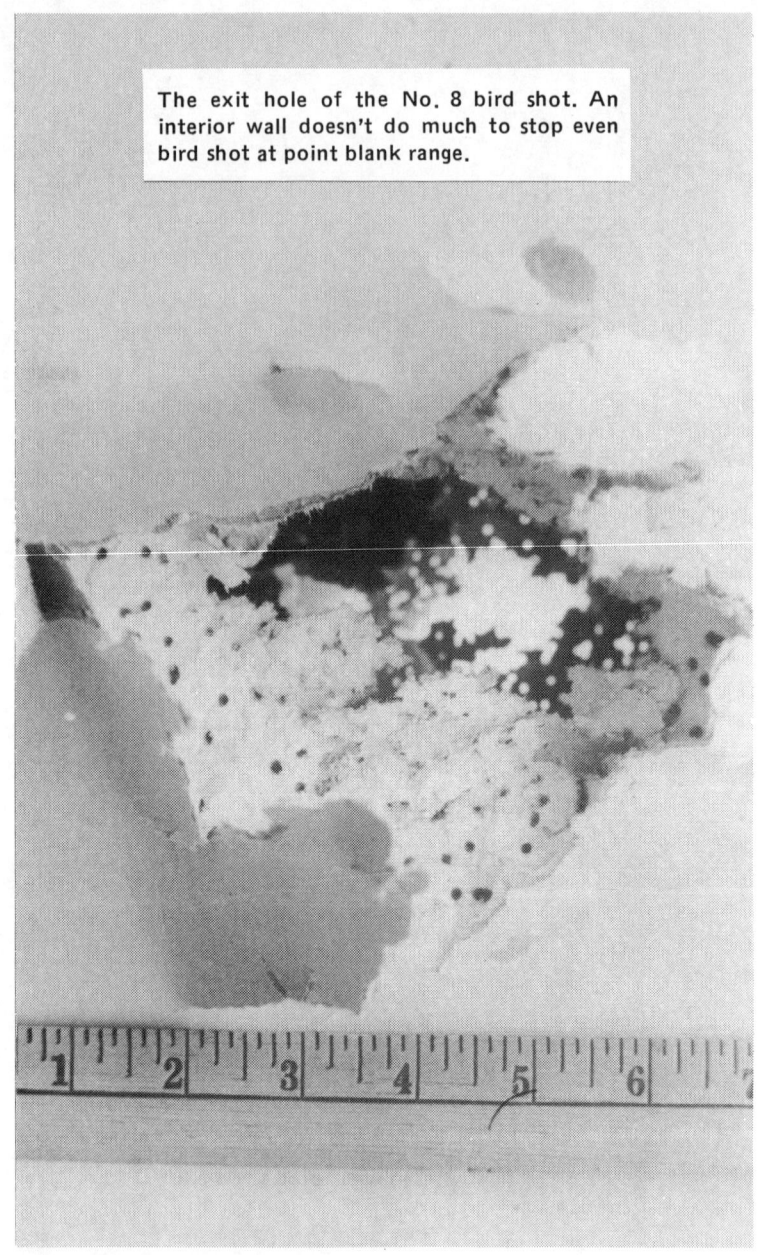

The exit hole of the No. 8 bird shot. An interior wall doesn't do much to stop even bird shot at point blank range.

THE SHOTGUN IN COMBAT

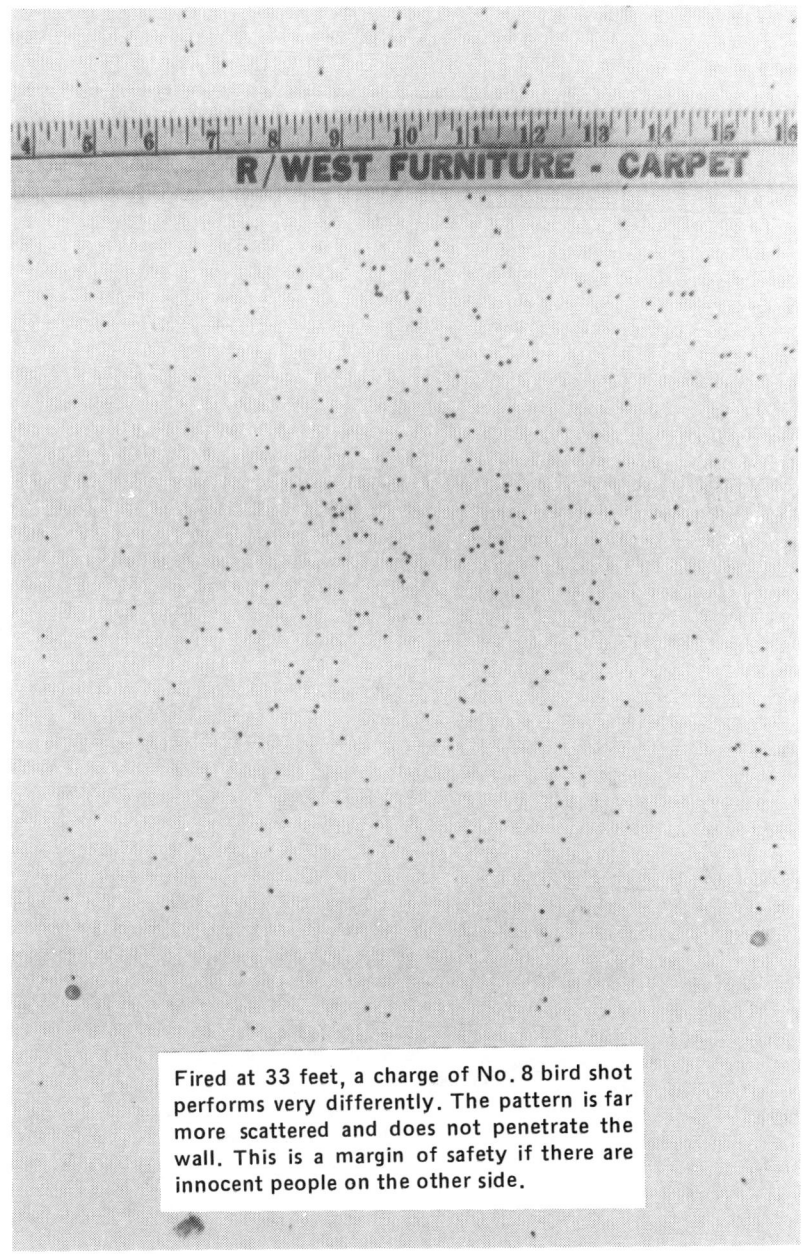

Fired at 33 feet, a charge of No. 8 bird shot performs very differently. The pattern is far more scattered and does not penetrate the wall. This is a margin of safety if there are innocent people on the other side.

THE SHOTGUN IN COMBAT

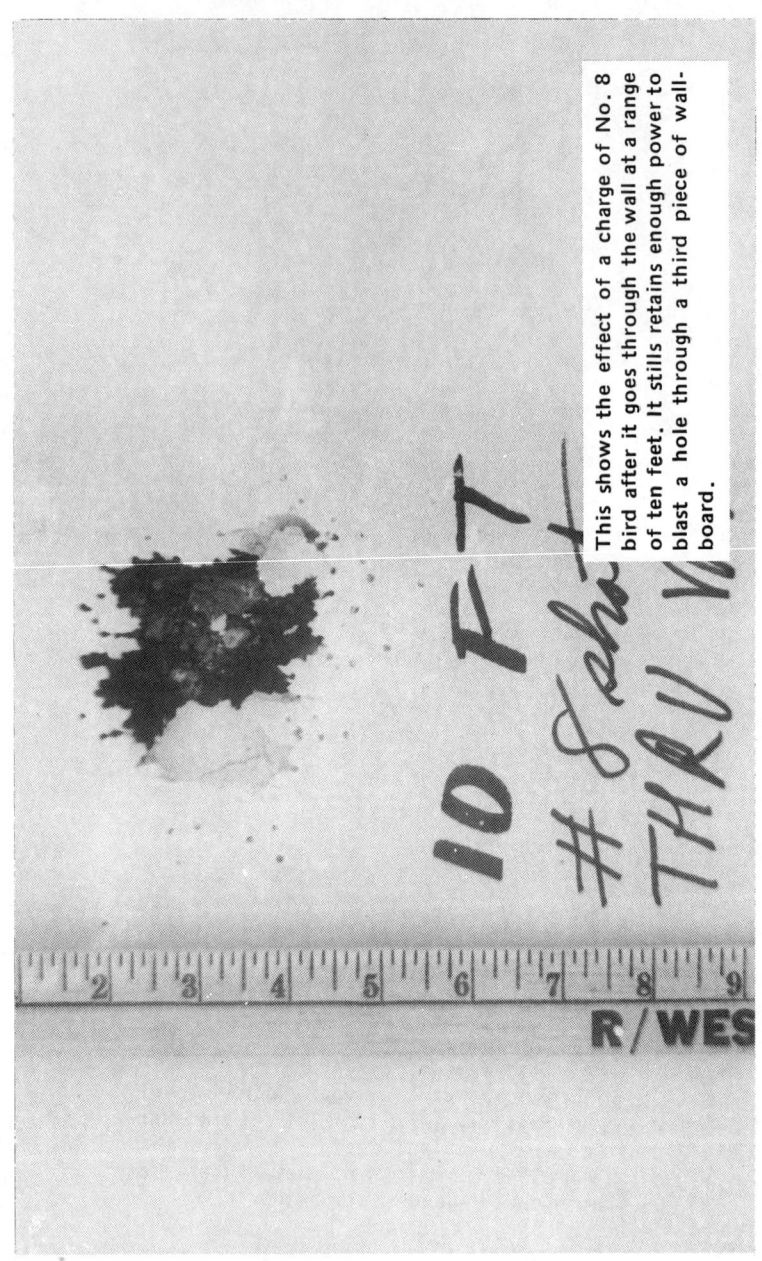

This shows the effect of a charge of No. 8 bird after it goes through the wall at a range of ten feet. It stills retains enough power to blast a hole through a third piece of wallboard.

#4 BUCK
THRU WALL
AND BOARD
20 FT. BEYOND

This piece of wallboard was placed twenty feet beyond the wall section. The charge of No. 4 buck went through the wall and penetrated this piece of wallboard in a wide pattern.

THE SHOTGUN IN COMBAT

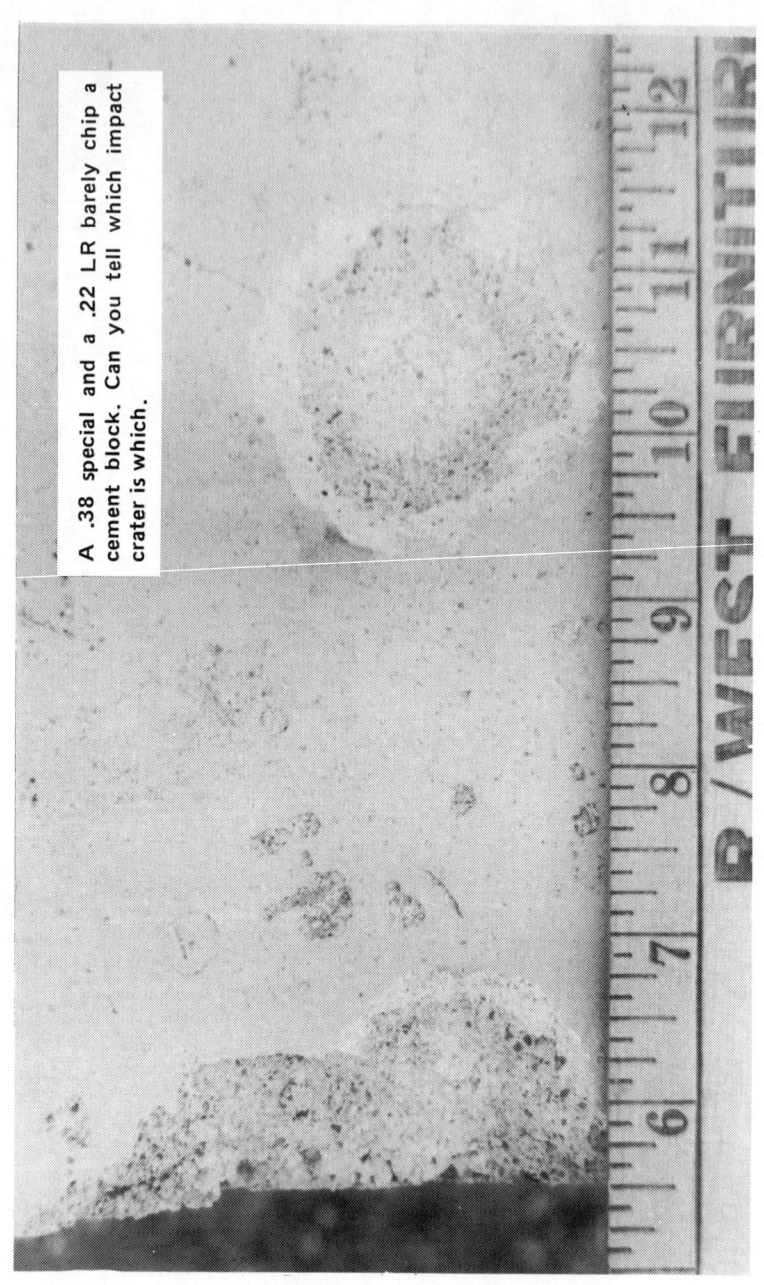

A .38 special and a .22 LR barely chip a cement block. Can you tell which impact crater is which.

THE SHOTGUN IN COMBAT

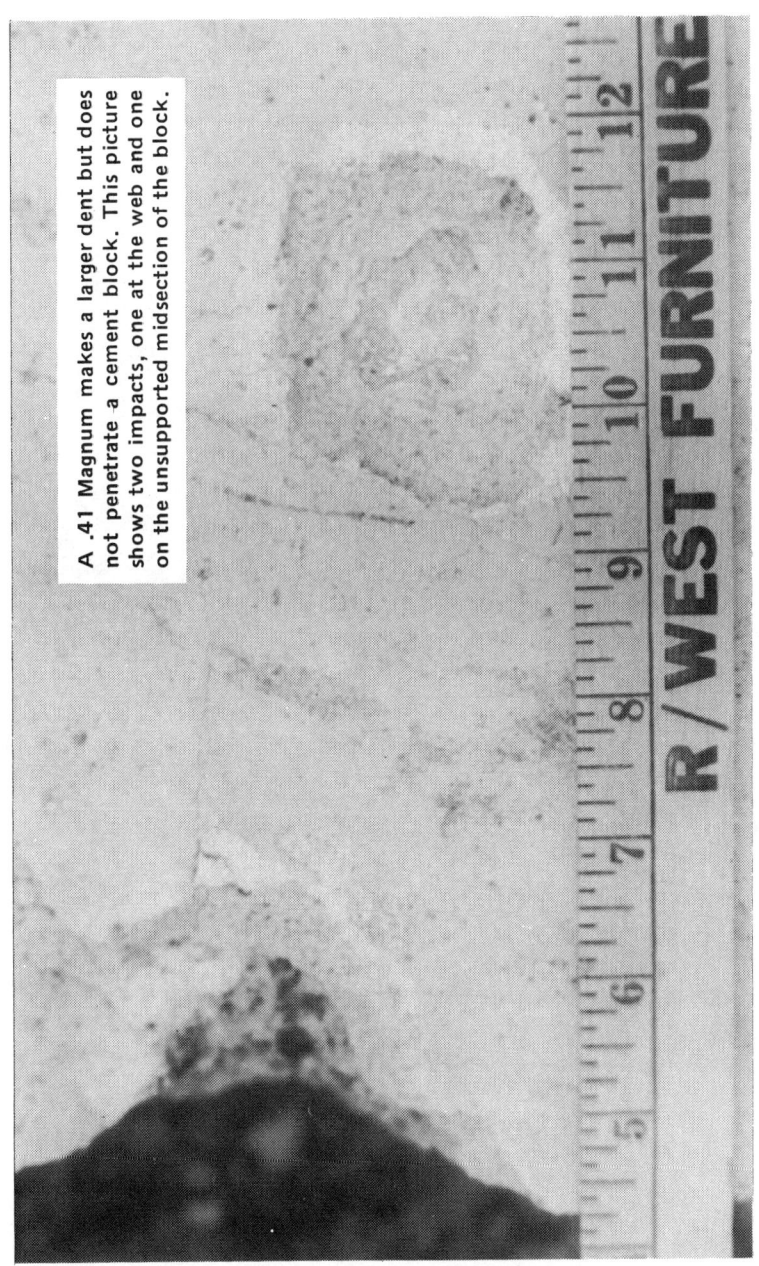

A .41 Magnum makes a larger dent but does not penetrate a cement block. This picture shows two impacts, one at the web and one on the unsupported midsection of the block.

THE SHOTGUN IN COMBAT

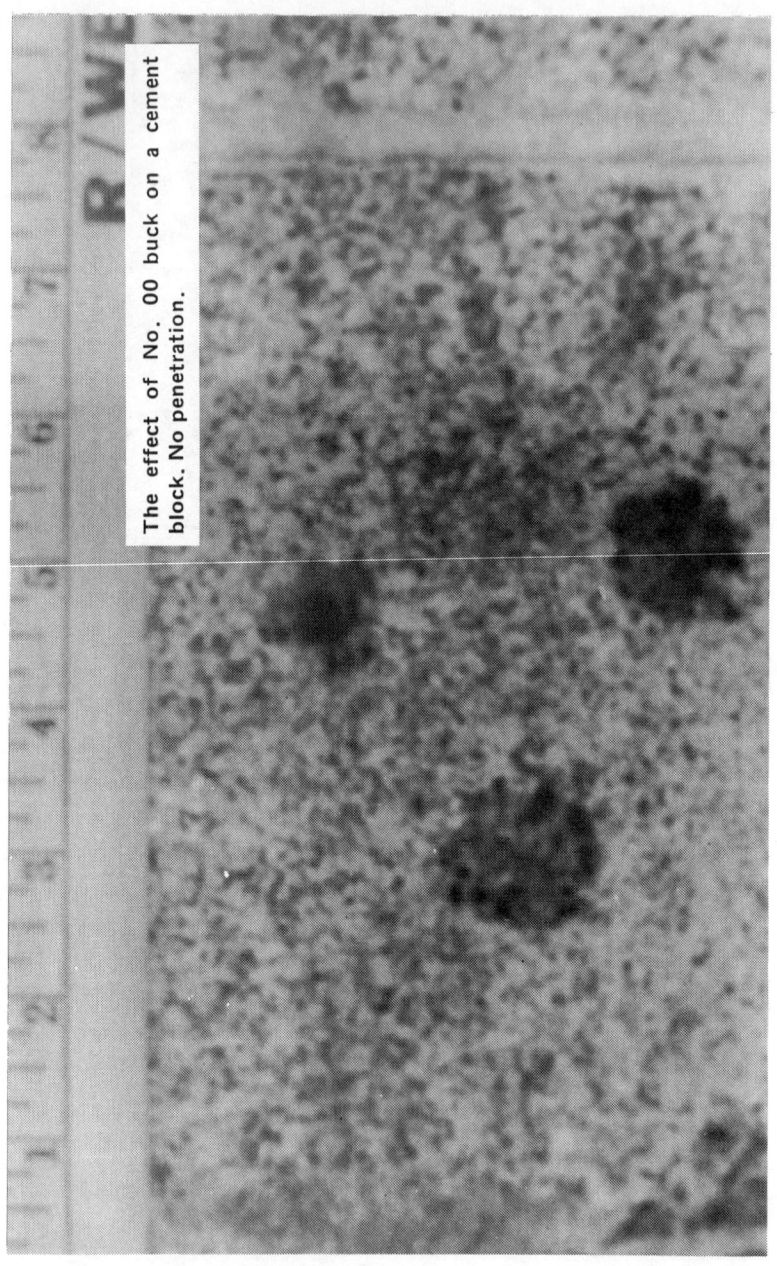

The effect of No. 00 buck on a cement block. No penetration.

THE SHOTGUN IN COMBAT

The combined impacts of No. 4 buck and No. 8 bird shot on a cement block. The shot scratched the surface, that's all.

A twelve gauge rifled slug broke the block when it hit the unsupported midsection. Whether it would go through both sides of a block which was a part of a wall is another question.

THE SHOTGUN IN COMBAT

The result of a slug fired at point blank range at another block so that it hit in the unsupported area between the webs. The block is shattered but the slug was found a few feet in front of the block, flattened out.

The same block, after a hit right on the web, the strongest part of the block. Again, no penetration. The slug finished up in front of the block and flattened out to about an inch diameter. Cement fragments flew behind the block, indicating that a person standing behind that block would have been shielded from the slug itself but would have been peppered with flying cement fragments.

THE SHOTGUN IN COMBAT

The result of firing a nine mm. metal piercing round into the cement block. The slug imbedded itself into the cement but did not penetrate or even shatter the block. In this case, as in the other tests against a cement block, there is no doubt that successive hits would have shattered the block and penetrated. Hardly any type of wall is absolute proof against sustained gunfire.

Shotgun Wounds

It is generally accepted that a shotgun produces fearsome wounds. This is generally true, due to the heavy charge weight, but a careful exploration of the mechanism of wounding is needed to understand precisely why and to recognize the exceptions.

Most people understand that a projectile passing through the human body produces a hole, technically known as the "permanent cavity." What is not so well understood is that if the projectile is moving at considerable speed it also produces a shock effect and an actual displacement of tissue known as the "temporary cavity", which collapses after the missile has passed through. The displaced tissue is definitely damaged but this may not be obvious to the casual observer.

The speed of the missile is all-important. A knife or pike-wound will not have a temporary cavity. A bullet wound will, due to the far greater speed of the missile. The U.S. Army tests demonstrated that the size of the temporary cavity is in proportion to the kinetic energy of the missile, which in turn is proportional to its speed. In simple language, a small fast missile will produce a larger temporary cavity than a large slow one.

The seriousness of the wound is proportional to the size of the temporary cavity, all other things being equal. It is obvious, of course, that a rifle bullet in the calf is not as serious as a pistol bullet in the brain, although the rifle bullet may destroy more tissue.

A distinction must be made between tissue destruction and tissue disruption. The permanent cavity results in tissue destruction, that is, a plug of tissue is pushed out ahead of the missile, or is pulped by the pressure of the bullet passing through. This is easy to understand, and there is little question as to the wounding power of the missile. What is more subtle is tissue disruption, and this is little understood, even by some medical men. Sometimes it is referred to as "shock," a misnomer which further confuses the issue. The tissue disruption can cause loss of function of the organ involved.

THE SHOTGUN IN COMBAT

This goes by different names, such as paralysis, mortification, and shock, but the result is the same. The tissue or organ stops working, either temporarily or permanently.

Another very important factor in determining wounding power is the number of missiles penetrating the body. Multiple hits are effective out of proportion to their number, in fact the destructive power is proportional to the square of their number. A quick look at a simple example will give an idea of the magnitude of the injuries we are considering. A charge of No. 00 buckshot, nine pellets travelling at over 1000 feet per second, measuring one third of an inch in diameter each, and hitting at point blank range with over two hundred foot-pounds of energy each, creates nine different wounds, each one approximately as serious as that made by a pistol bullet. In practical terms a hit in the torso with such a charge is usually fatal.

Many attempts have been made to quantify the power of firearms with formulas pertaining to "stopping power." None of the various efforts made so far seems to be satisfactory, as each year brings forth a new expert with a new formula or a new modification of an old one. None of these numbers games is completely satisfactory because they all deal with an abstraction, rather than real events. No consideration of wounding or stopping power can be accurate without specifying the site of the hit. It is obvious that not all areas of the human body are equally vulnerable or vital to life.

Also ignored is the question of whether the missile strikes soft tissue or bone. If it strikes bone the impact breaks off pieces of bone which go off in different directions and create their own wound channels. These secondary missiles, as they are called, generate an effect like a miniature shotgun blast. It is an irony of the design of the human body that the ribs, which serve as armor around the vital organs of the upper torso and which will deflect blows or even stabbing injuries, serve only to enhance the effect of a bullet wound in this area.

The production of secondary missiles depends on the momentum of the primary missile, that is, mass times speed, and not kinetic energy. The shotgun, because it fires a very

THE SHOTGUN IN COMBAT

heavy charge compared to other weapons, excells in this area. Typically, the charge is an ounce or more of lead, which is heavy indeed compared to the bullets fired from rifled weapons.

Vulnerability Of The Human Body

There are many points on the human body which are more vulnerable than others to injury. Those which particularly concern us here are those which comprise a vital part of the life support systems of the body.

The body can sustain severe injuries without being disabled or killed. An arm or a leg can be blown off and yet death may not come immediately. If the person in question is your opponent he might well be able to keep firing at you.

The following sketches give a rough guide to the most vulnerable points, vulnerable in the sense that their injury or destruction is immediately life-threatening. For example, it is easy to see that a pellet of double-ought in the brain will do more immediate harm than one in the large intestine. In the latter case, peritonitis and blood poisoning would follow, but they are not immediately fatal. The pain would be intense, particularly after several hours, but by that time the gunfight would have long been settled.

We must mention two cautions. First, the following sketches are imprecise because the human body is imprecise. Everyone is built differently and the size and location of any organ will vary somewhat from person to person. Moreover, some organs are not tied down and do move according to the position of the body. The brain is always in the same place but the heart will wander a few centimeters depending upon whether the person is lying down, standing, running, etc. The lungs vary in size from moment to moment, with each breath.

Secondly, the sketches show frontal views. The apparent position of an organ within the body changes with the view. For example the spine is seen to be at the midline of the torso in the frontal view. A person standing in profile would have the spine at one side or the other.

You cannot hope to aim at a specific organ in a gunfight. Fortunately, with a shotgun such precision is unnecessary. The scatter of the pellets enhances the destructive effect by involving several organs. Using the upper torso as the aim

THE SHOTGUN IN COMBAT

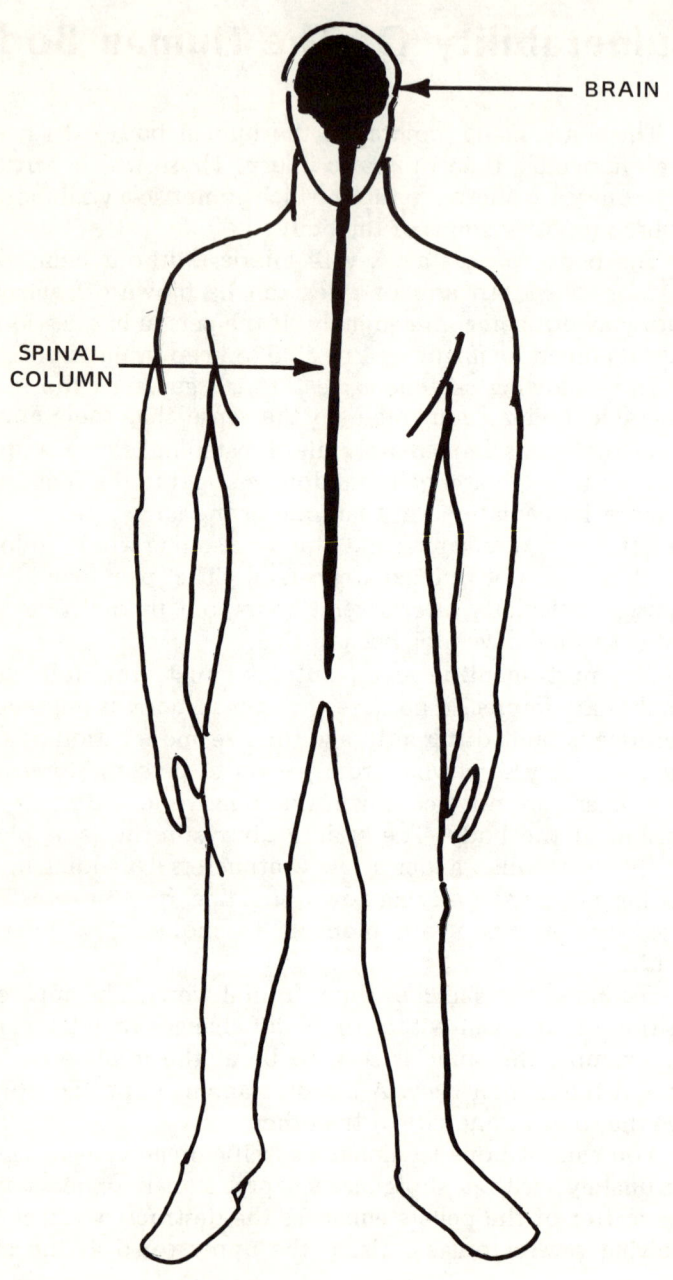

THE SHOTGUN IN COMBAT

THE CENTRAL NERVOUS SYSTEM

The brain and the spinal cord are the most vulnerable points here. A hit in the brain will cause immediate unconsciousness and rapid death, unless the victim is very, very lucky. While there are occasional cases of people surviving gunshot wounds of the brain it is a rare thing.

The brain is well protected. It is in an armored casing, the skull. While a bullet will penetrate the skull some of the light shot, such as No. 8 fired at a distance, would not. Of course, double-ought and No. 4 buck will.

The spinal cord is also armored except for the part within the neck. The bones which comprise the vertebrae protect the cable of nerves from casual blows and mishaps. Nevertheless the spinal cord is exposed at the back of the neck before it reaches the skull. To reach the spine a bullet or shotgun pellet must travel through the thickness of the torso when fired from the front. This offers a lot of protection and only the heavier missiles will penetrate enough. A hit in the cervical spine, that part within the neck, is fatal as it cuts the nerve controlling the heartbeat and respiration.

It is possible, of course, to hit the specific nerve controlling the heart between the spine and the heart itself but as a practical matter this can be ignored. It is easier to hit the heart itself and the result is just as fatal.

Hits on the nervous system as described are about as close as it is possible to come to guaranteeing instant incapacitation. Other parts of the nervous system, such as the nerves controlling the legs, are vulnerable if hit but they are impossible as targets because they are too hard to pinpoint and hit in a shootout. In any event, a shotgun would not only affect the nerve but would pulp the tissue around it for several inches.

THE SHOTGUN IN COMBAT

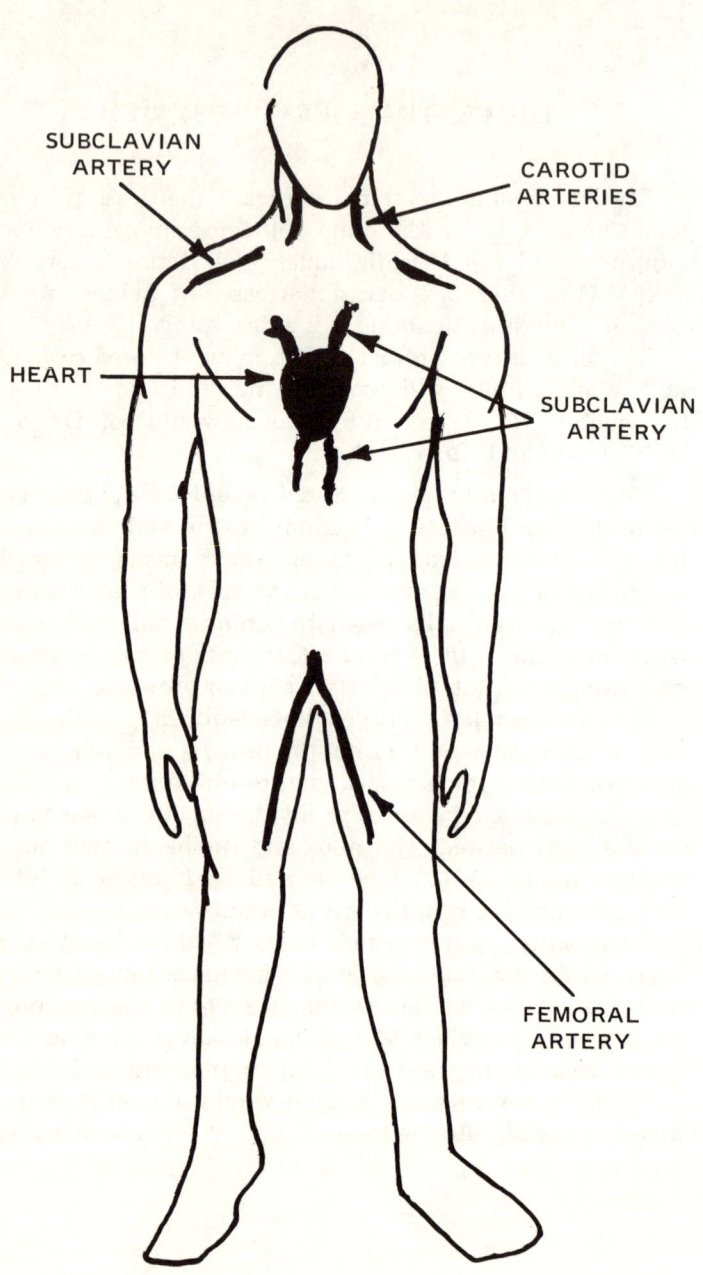

THE SHOTGUN IN COMBAT

THE CIRCULATORY SYSTEM

The heart is the big pump, of course. It lies in a protected position within the rib cage but is vulnerable to gunfire. It is a tempting target because you do not have to hit the heart to cause a fatal injury. A near miss can still hit the vena cava and the aorta, the major blood vessels leading to and from the heart, causing a fatal hemorrhage. With a hit on the heart unconsciousness occurs within a few seconds and death within four minutes. A hit on the blood vessels does not always result in such rapid effects but the chances of surviving such a wound are nil, as you cannot put a tourniquet on a blood vessel buried within the chest.

The subclavian arteries are somewhat protected by the clavicle, the collar bone, but a gunshot can break through them. Again, they are in an inaccessible position so that if you rupture one a fatal hemorrhage occurs.

The carotid arteries, on either side of the neck, are wide open to light bird shot or even a knife thrust. Near each carotid artery is the jugular vein, which leads blood back from the brain. Generally, a hit with a shotgun which gets one will get them all since they are so close together.

The effect is immediate and profound. With the severing of the carotid arteries the blood supply to the brain stops and the victim becomes unconscious within a few seceonds. Death follows within a few minutes, usually four.

The femoral arteries, in the insides of the thighs, supply the legs with blood. They are unprotected except for soft tissue and are very vulnerable. A hit in the femoral artery can cause the victim to bleed to death within a few minutes. The incapacitating effect is not as immediate as a hit on another part of the circulatory system but the end is the same if the wound is left untreated. A tourniquet can be put around the thigh, however, and if needed direct pressure will stop the bleeding. This is hard to do in the middle of a gunfight, however.

THE SHOTGUN IN COMBAT

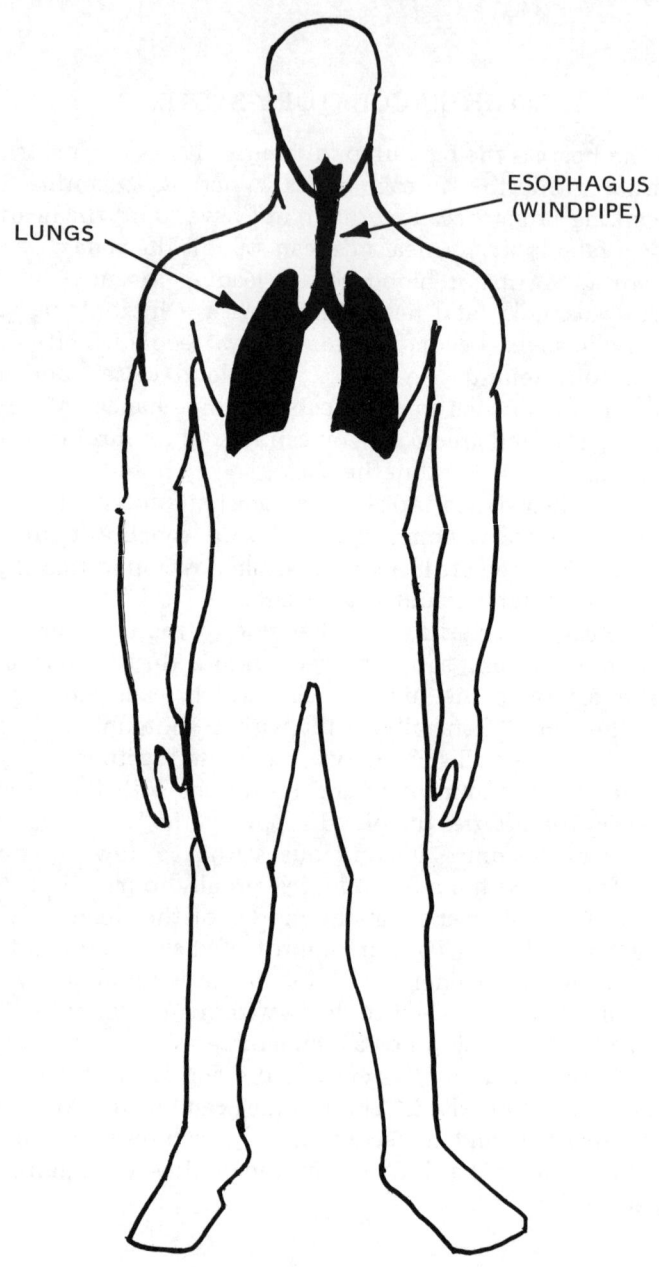

THE SHOTGUN IN COMBAT

THE RESPIRATORY SYSTEM

The windpipe is the most vulnerable but the effect can be disappointing, as a puncture will not stop the victim from getting air. However, a wound in the neck with a shotgun rarely involves the esophagus alone and the windpipe can easily become obstructed with blood, impairing respiration. The lungs are protected by the rib cage, as is the heart, but a shotgun blast will break through and cause multiple punctures. This will prejudice the victim's survival in two ways.

The first is by the punctures themselves, which will admit air and cause the collapse of the lung. With the lung collapsed the intake of air is obstructed and asphyxiation follows.

The second is the massive bleeding. The lungs are well supplied with blood and projectiles tearing up lung tissue will also tear up many large and small blood vessels. The lungs will then flood with blood, impeding ventilation and causing asphyxiation.

THE SHOTGUN IN COMBAT

point and assuming a ten-inch pattern it is easy to see how the respiratory system, the central nervous system, and the circulatory system will be gravely affected. In fact, it is hard to see how it is possible to survive such a wound.

Apart from structural damage to vital organs the body can be disabled from pain and shock. Pain is not always a major factor as the impact has a numbing action on the nerves and it has happened often that people have been shot without a subjective sensation of great pain but rather a feeling of having been struck with a hammer. Pain is not a reliable effect of gunshot wounds.

Shock is a complicated subject. Psychological shock can be as paralyzing as the most severe physical shock. Some people react to great danger by total inhibition of any action. They are pschologically paralyzed with fright, as the expression goes.

Neural shock results in local paralysis. The effect is familiar to anyone who has hit his "funny-bone." A missile striking near a nerve can put it out of action permanently or temporarily. Of course, if it cuts the nerve the effect is immediate and permanent. A hit in a muscle will usually paralyze that muscle through a combination of tissue destruction and neural shock.

Finally there is physiological shock. This one is a killer. Basically it is overloading the body's defenses. A severe hemorrhage that results in lowered blood pressure, shallow respiration, and irregular heartbeat means shock and this process usually hastens death. Shock usually results in unconsciousness shortly after its onset.

Shock can appear quickly after wounding, if the wound is severe or it may occur slowly in the case of lesser wounds. In its severe form the blood vessels dilate, lowering blood pressure. The heartbeat becomes irregular and the victim collapses. Unconsciousness and death quickly follow.

The more systems injured the more quickly shock will follow and the more severe the effect. There are significant exceptions, however. A slight wound, coupled with extreme fright, can cause a combatant to faint. People have been

THE SHOTGUN IN COMBAT

known to faint from a tooth extraction or a severely cut finger. A gunshot wound is more serious than that and the effect can be expected to be enhanced somewhat.

Advantages And Disadvantages Of The Shotgun

Like any mechanical contrivance, whether it be a firearm, lawnmower or kitchen appliance, shotguns are designed for a specific purpose. There are certain advantages and disadvantages to selecting a shotgun over a rifle or handgun; but the advantages listed below easily outweigh the disadvantages.

Stopping Power: Certain writers tout the .45 ACP or the .44 Magnum as the ultimate in handgun stopping power. But as the photos in this text indicate, even the tiny No. 8 or No. 9 shot will produce a nasty wound at close ranges; one that will most assuredly stop an adversary in his tracks. With a load of 00 or No. 4 buckshot, the wound would be truly devastating even at longer ranges. As an example, the famous train robber of the early 1900's, Black Jack Ketchum, had his right arm literally blown off by a blast from a shotgun in the hands of an alert express car guard.

Intimidation: In many cases, such as apprehending a burglar in a residence in the middle of the night, the mere presence of a shotgun will often do the trick. No one in his right mind would willingly risk being shot with one at close range; the average burglar would probably stand meekly while the shotgun wielding householder picked up the telephone and called the police.

They may lack the firepower of a submachine gun, but they are far safer for innocent bystanders since they have a shorter range and lesser penetration. The value of a shotgun in such situations has long been appreciated and they were always the preferred weapon of frontier marshals who had to face an angry lynch mob.

Lesser Legal Restrictions: In many Eastern cities, it is becoming virtually impossible for the average citizen to legally purchase a handgun for home defense. The trend started with New York's notorious Sullivan law which has had no effect on crime except to assure the criminal element that they have

THE SHOTGUN IN COMBAT

an unarmed public upon which to prey. Some cities also have licensing and registration requirements on shotguns and rifles, but the authorities are far less likely to refuse a request for a license to own a shotgun than for one to own a handgun. The latter are looked upon as "no good for anything but killing somebody" while the former are recognized as being primarily sporting arms. Of course, either type of gun can be used for recreation or as an instrument of death, but the average citizen in a large city who wants a gun for protection will encounter fewer problems if he chooses a shotgun. Ironically, some of the politicians who favor registration or outright confiscation of handguns own and use shotguns for recreational purposes.

Easier Shot Placement: Due to the spreading of the shot pattern, point of aim is not as critical with a shotgun as with a rifle or handgun. At ten feet or so, the shot will not spread enough to make this a critical factor. As the distance from shooter to target increases, so does the likelihood of missing with a pistol. With a shotgun, the increase in distance creates a corresponding increase in the spread of the shot pattern. Whereas a near miss with a pistol is just that, a near miss; a near miss with a shotgun would assure that some of the pellets would still strike the target.

Availability of Ammunition: Immediately following the ever popular .22 long rifle, 12 gauge shotgun shells are probably among the most readily available ammunition today. The average sporting goods store will stock a large variety of rifle and pistol ammunition in just about every conceivable factory loading, but Cousin Eb's general store at Podunk Hollow cannot afford to stock such a variety. They may need to limit their handgun stock to the popular .38 Special and .357 Magnum offerings. Depending on the area, .30-30 or .30-06 rifle ammunition may be about all they stock, but just about any store in the country that stocks any ammunition will have one or two 12 gauge loads to offer. They may not stock your particular pet load, but they will have something that will fit your scattergun.

Versatility: The person who must limit himself to one gun for all purposes either due to economic factors or storage

THE SHOTGUN IN COMBAT

problems would do well to consider the shotgun. It has adequate stopping power for home defense. It is ideal for hunting waterfowl. Properly loaded, it is suitable for pest control. In areas where game laws permit, deer can be taken with buckshot or rifled slugs. Indeed, some areas which have a fairly dense rural population permit deer hunting only with shotguns since their shorter range offers a decided safety advantage over high-powered rifles. Although not suited for informal plinking, which is basically the realm of the .22, the shotgun can still be pressed into service for this type of shooting. Many shotguns can be fitted with an adjustable choke device which enables you to alter the choke for a particular shotshell load in a matter of seconds. Some guns, particularly of the bolt action variety, have these devices installed at the factory.

Although shotguns are slower to reload than an automatic pistol or a revolver, this is generally not a critical factor in combat situations. Police statistics indicate that the average combatant will fire less than three shots in a gunfight. A pump or autoloading shotgun which holds five or six rounds should be more than adequate for defense purposes.

While the bulk and weight of a shotgun preclude the average police officer carrying one as a matter of course, and they are definitely out of the question for an undercover agent who must have a weapon that is easily concealed, they can be carried in the trunk of a patrol car. They are out of the way, yet available if the officer has adequate warning that he may need something more powerful or threatening than his regulation .38. In many cases where an officer is called in to face a potential shoot-out there is adequate time for him to get the shotgun out of the trunk before proceeding to the scene.

At distances of a couple of hundred yards or more, both the pistol and shotgun are far outclassed by a high-powered scoped rifle. However, instances where a sniper is needed to knock out an antagonist at a great distance are few and far between and need not be considered here. But for many defense situations, either involving police or the householder in his own home, the shotgun offers a better than average if not always ideal solution.

Basic Combat Use Of The Shotgun

The shotgun is basically a shoulder weapon. Skeet and trap shooters and hunters all use the shotgun from the orthodox firing position, for good reason. In a combat situation the best tactic may be to use the shotgun from the hip position, depending on the situation. Often, if the target is close enough and there is a need for haste, shooting from the hip is the method of choice. If your target is farther away and precision is important, bring the shotgun up to your shoulder if time allows. Often, a compromise will be all you can do. Fortunately, a shotgun lends itself well to compromise because of its great firepower. Keep in mind that it can deliver a nasty kick if not well seated against your shoulder.

A shotgun should never be used alone if you can avoid it. Some are single shots and others have a rather limited magazine capacity. Mitigating this is the fact that they usually do the job with the first shot, if you hit. However, shotguns are slow to reload, whatever the make and type, and a pistol on your hip as a backup will give you some peace of mind.

An exception to this principle is the home defense situation. If you are awakened in the middle of the night by an intruder you will have all you can do to get your shotgun into your hand and your family to safety (if there is time) without worrying about a pistol. This is true even if all you have is a single shot.

If you are a police officer you will be carrying a sidearm as a matter of course. So do some military personnel. Whatever the case, if at all possible, carry a pistol as insurance against those disturbing moments when you run out of ammunition in your magazine or the gun jams. It may make a big difference to you someday.

NON-LETHAL USE OF THE SHOTGUN

Just as the pistol can be used as a club, the shotgun can be used to inflict disabling, but non-lethal, injuries upon an opponent. Since the shotgun is normally grasped with both hands you can put a lot of power into a swing. The shotgun

THE SHOTGUN IN COMBAT

can be used to deflect a blow from a club or a knife. It can be used to pin an opponent against a wall and choke him. Finally, there is the military butt-swing.

The military butt-swing is used to subdue one or a number of opponents in a smooth, rhythmic sequence of strokes. It originally came from the use of the bayonet but it works well even without a blade on the end of the barrel. The first step is to jab the barrel into the adversary's stomach. Then bring the butt up smartly into his face or chin. The final step is to slam the butt into the back of his head on the downstroke. The illustrations accompanying this chapter show the sequence of steps clearly.

With the proliferation of schools teaching judo, karate and other forms of unarmed combat, there is a distinct possibility of encountering an expert who will take the gun away from you with his bare hands and make you eat it, or worse. That is why closing with an opponent is mainly a last desperate measure. It should only be attempted if and when you have run out of ammunition and are surprised before you can draw your pistol, or if your opponent is not very formidable.

If you do wind up trying to put down an adversary with the military butt-swing and he does succeed in taking it away from you, the best course of action is to let go of the weapon before he expects you to, back off, draw your pistol and shoot him. It is best to give no warning. You are fighting for your life and if you waste time by saying "Drop it!" he may drop you instead.

SUPPRESSIVE FIRE

"Suppressive Fire" is a term that is often used to denote massive spraying in the general direction of the enemy. This is usually a measure of desperation employed when time is short, the enemy cannot be seen clearly, and/or there is a need to cover movement. The term "covering fire" is perhaps more appropriate in the last situation. Covering fire can be aimed as well as just pointed, and it does serve to

THE SHOTGUN IN COMBAT

force the enemy to keep his head down while you or members of your party change positions.

It is extremely important to conserve ammunition because a shotgun is so slow to reload. On the other hand, because of the patterning of shotgun fire, it is easier to hit a target with a shotgun than with a single projectile weapon. Even this has its limitations, however. Shotgun fire should still be aimed whenever possible.

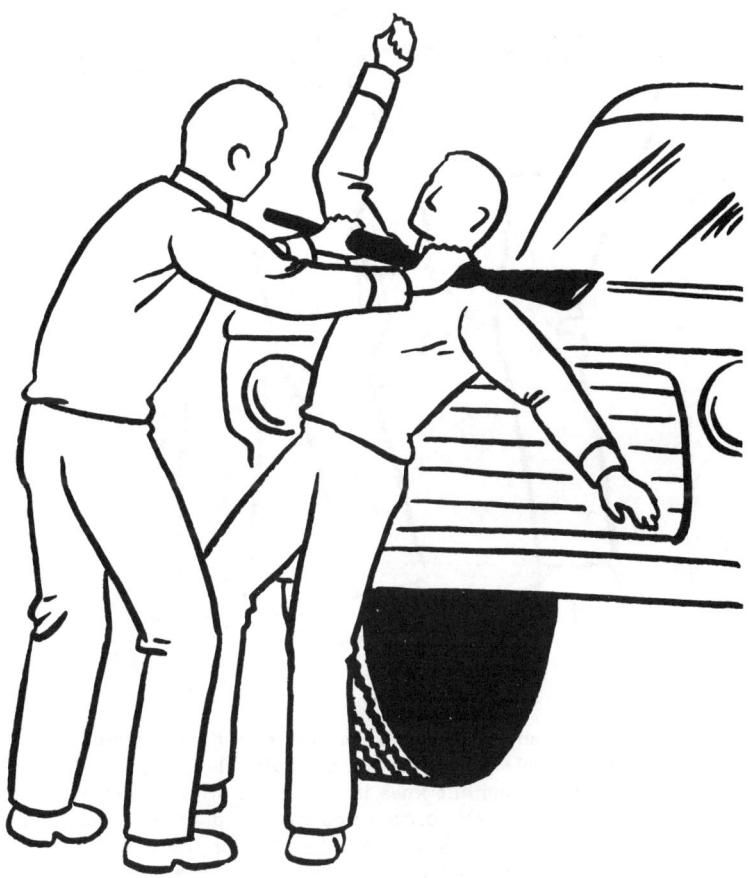

The front strangle. Backing an opponent up against a wall or some other unyielding object and putting the barrel to his throat can be very persuasive at times.

THE SHOTGUN IN COMBAT

The rear strangle. This requires a bit more coordination but it is potentially more effective. Dropping the barrel over his head and putting one knee in his back will bend him over backward, in which position you can complete the strangle or break his neck if you give a sharp tug on the shotgun. It is important to break your opponent's balance by that jab in the back with your knee otherwise he might grab the barrel, bend forward, and dump you forward over his head.

THE SHOTGUN IN COMBAT

Blocking the overhead knife thrust. Use the barrel or forestock of the shotgun to break the force of the blow. It is important to catch him at the top of the stroke, before he has built up any momentum, which would make it harder to stop the thrust.

THE SHOTGUN IN COMBAT

The wrong way. Letting him get too close before striking can get you a nasty wound even as you lunge to parry his blow. The shotgun gives you extra reach. Use it!

THE SHOTGUN IN COMBAT

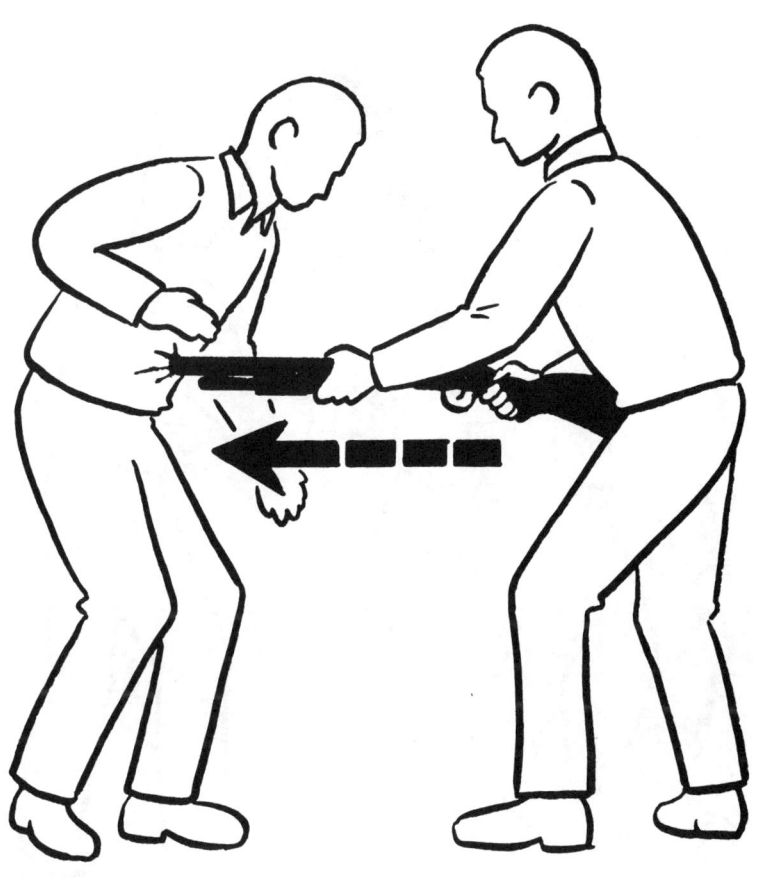

The right way. Using your extra reach and jabbing hard into the midsection will certainly discourage your opponent.

THE SHOTGUN IN COMBAT

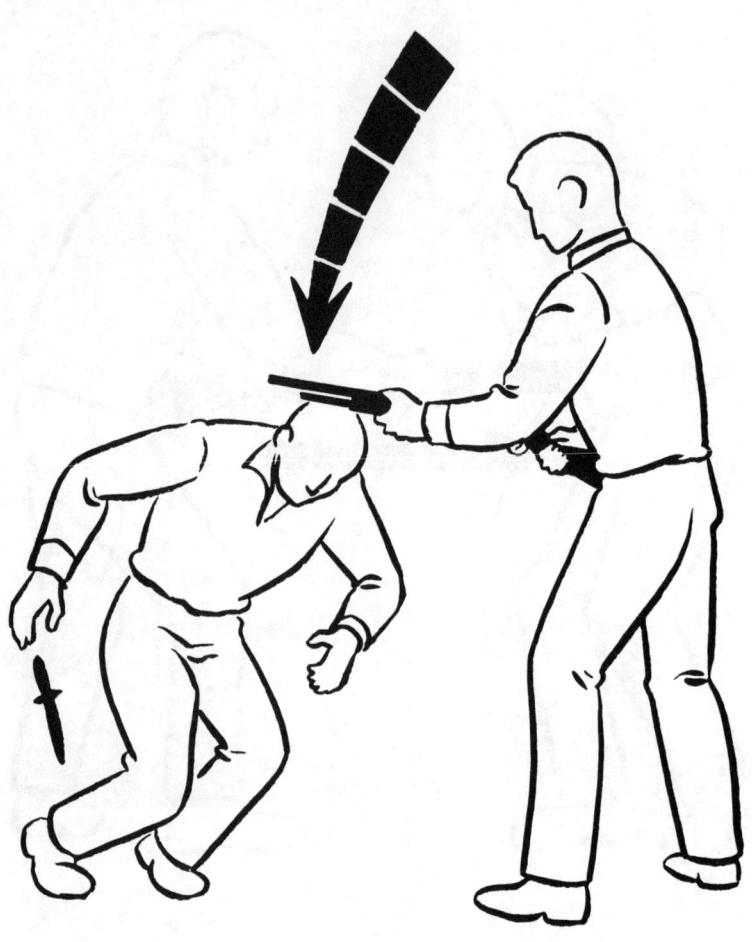

Following up with a crunch to the head will put him down for good.

THE SHOTGUN IN COMBAT

When faced by an opponent with a knife shoot him immediately or if you cannot, keep him from closing in to the range of his weapon. Make him keep his distance with short jabs from your shotgun until you can strike more effectively. Be ready to parry or to block blows.

THE SHOTGUN IN COMBAT

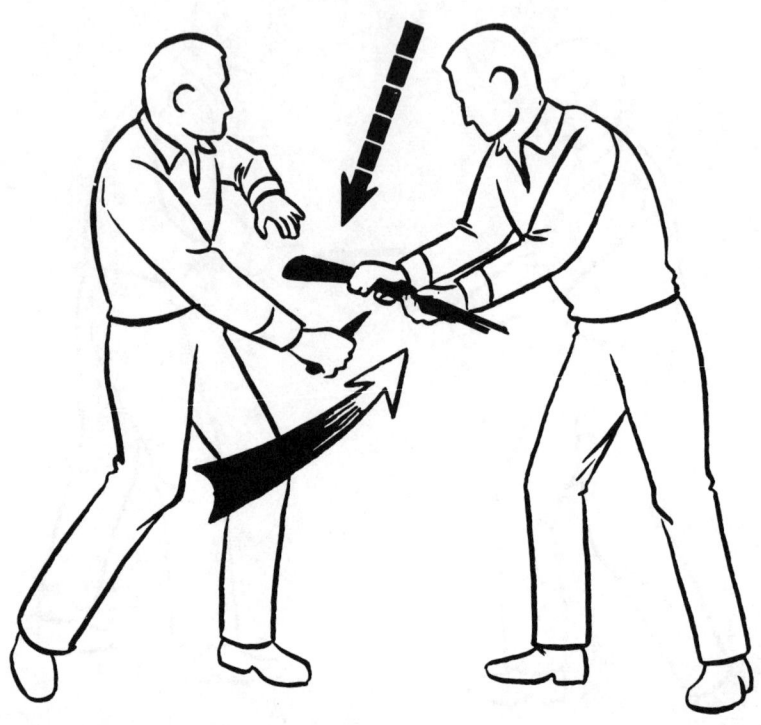

This requires a block. Reach out and meet him more than halfway. Once you have stopped his thrust, stamp on his foot.

THE SHOTGUN IN COMBAT

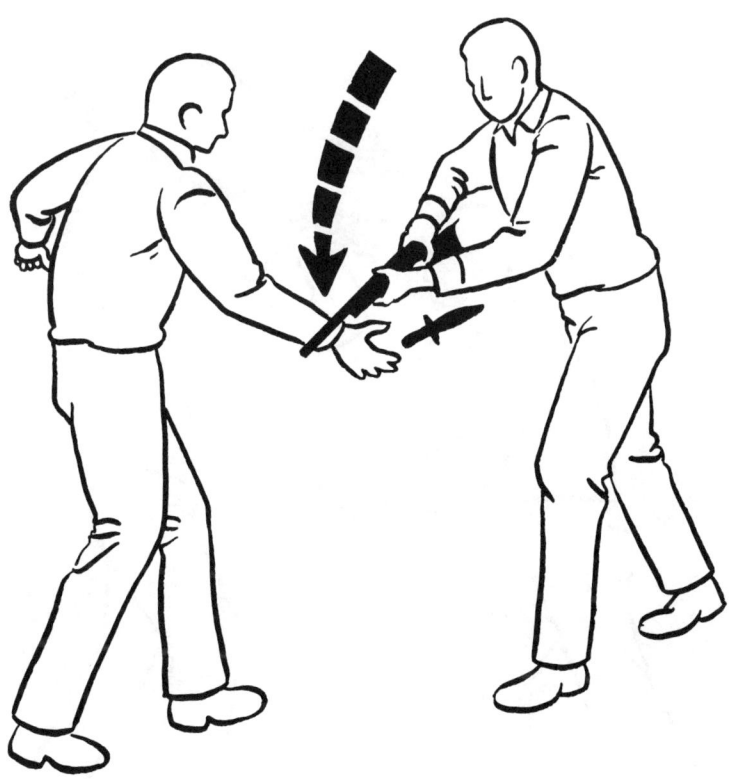

Parrying a thrust. This is both a parry and a counterblow. You can make your parry hard enough to make him drop his knife or you might just wish to deflect it so that you can step in close and give him a knee in the groin.

THE SHOTGUN IN COMBAT

The wrong way to do it. You might crack his skull this way but in trying you leave yourself wide open. If he ducks his head and plunges that knife into you, you're in trouble.

THE SHOTGUN IN COMBAT

The first stage of the military butt-swing. Jab hard into his stomach. He starts to fold over.

THE SHOTGUN IN COMBAT

As his head is coming down, swing the butt into his chin or his face, hard.

THE SHOTGUN IN COMBAT

As he's going down follow through on the upswing and then reverse and bring the butt down on his head, finishing him off. As you follow through on this one you'll bring the gun level again as in a previous picture, ready to tackle the next opponent, if any.

A Quick Review Of Basic Tactics

Proficiency with a firearm is not quite as important as sound tactics in combat. With poor tactics you can throw away whatever advantage you have in marksmanship over youropponent. Some of the basic principles to use are:

Cover and concealment. If time permits, use them.

Visibility. This is not quite the same as cover or concealment. Try to take up a position where you are not well illuminated and your opponent is. Deep shadows can give you an advantage of a couple of seconds before your opponent sees you. If you, on the other hand, let yourself be silhouetted or brightly illuminated while your adversary remains in obscurity you are at a disadvantage. You throw away the next advantage, surprise.

Surprise. This should be self-explanatory but unfortunately it isn't. While it is obvious that the one who takes his opponent by surprise has the advantage there are complications. If you can have the advantage of surprise you can get the first shot and, presumably, the first hit. This may bring you into conflict with the law in certain circumstances. Generally, unless you are in your own home, you cannot fire first and ask questions later. There are many if, ands, and buts to this question and no generalizations can be made except to plead the cause of hard-core realism. Survival comes first and foremost. It is imcomparably better to be tried by twelve than carried by six.

Fire or cover? This is often a dilemma. When in a firefight it can cost you a precious second or two while you decide whether to return fire first or seek cover first. The basic argument for seeking cover is so obvious that it need not even be put into words but the argument for returning fire first is slightly more subtle. If you shoot your opponent down you won't have to seek cover. The best, of course, is to shoot him down from cover but you usually don't have this priviledge unless you are lying in ambush. Whatever you do, you must do it with . . .

Speed. Don't procrastinate. Wasting time can cost you your life. Think, and use caution, but don't stall. Act on your

THE SHOTGUN IN COMBAT

decision immediately. What may have been a good move a few moments ago is a bad move now. However, don't let the need for speed interfere with your accuracy.

Accuracy. An oft-repeated cliche about gunfighting is; "Take your time, fast." What this means in less cryptic language is that you should strive to make every shot count. A slight delay while you make sure you're aimed right is better than a miss. If you miss your spot your opponent a shot. A rough average is a shot per second. A fraction of a second spent in steadying your aim is well spent. If you miss it can take you a second to jack another shell into the chamber and bring the shotgun down again for another round. During that time, he can blow you into orbit. Alternatively, he can decide that the enviroment is unhealthy and jump for cover.

Minimize your exposure. Don't fire long strings from the standing position or engage multiple opponents from the standing position. Don't stand up to reload or to clear a jam. When changing position run as fast as you can and keep low.

Never get caught with an empty gun. Whenever you get the chance slip a couple of shells into the magazine. At least have a pistol for backup.

Try to be aware of your opponent's ammunition situation. If he runs dry you can change your position or rush him while he is reloading.

Be aware that, if you hit your opponent, he might not be dead yet or he might even be faking. In a life and death situation you would be wise to let him have another load before breaking cover and approaching the body.

Last but not least, try to avoid situations in which you'll be outnumbered.

Using The Shotgun In Combat

When considering the shotgun for combat, two of its features stand out: its size and its power.

The shotgun is a large weapon, typically. It is not easily concealable, like a pistol which can be hidden in a pocket, under a shirt or a jacket. You need an overcoat to conceal a shotgun, and even an overcoat will not do if the barrel is too long. Some people adopt the expedient of sawing off their barrels to make the weapon more easy to hide. This defeats the purpose of a shotgun. When you shorten the barrel you lose power and you increase muzzle blast and flash. This tends to negate the purpose of the shotgun. If you want a pistol, get a pistol. Extensively modifying a shotgun is a bad way to do it.

With all that, there are some shotguns which are designed for easy concealability. Some take-down models are easy to hide under a coat but they require assembly before use. This may be a matter of a few seconds or it may require a screwdriver and several minutes' work. One model, the Remington 870P, has a folding skeleton stock. It can be fired with the stock folded or extended. The stock snaps open and locks in a second, which makes it a good choice for someone who needs a short, light, easily hidden shotgun.

The power of a shotgun, whether measured in weight of charge, momentum, or kinetic energy, is more that that of most other firearms. It is possible to find a super-powerful caliber and say that the .465 Super-Auto-Mangler has X foot-pounds more energy than a 12 gauge, but that is the exception and not the rule.

Shotguns vary in magazine capacity. There are single shots and there are "police-type" shotguns which hold up to eight in a tubular magazine. They all have one feature in common: they are slow to reload, compared to most pistols and some rifles. This is not as bad as it seems because most of the time one hit from a shotgun will do the same job as several hits from a pistol. Even a single shot shotgun must be taken seriously because if you hit with its one shot you

THE SHOTGUN IN COMBAT

probably won't need any follow-up shots. Of course, a lot depends upon the situation you are facing. A householder can feel secure with a single shot weapon but a police officer would surely prefer a magazine weapon.

Whatever the case may be, it is a good idea to have a pistol as a back-up weapon. It is not likely that you'll need it but if you do you'll need it very much.

One fine point that is neglected is to learn to use the shotgun one-handed. You may never have to but if you are wounded it is essential to be able to get along with only one hand. Many pistol shooters learn to shoot one-handed but for some indefinable reason shotgunners overlook this art.

Having a pistol is particularly important if your shotgun is a single shot or a double barrelled. You run out of ammunition very quickly with one of those, although if you hit your target well, you should not need any follow-up shots. Still, it is comforting to have a pistol on your person just is case.

The ideal shotgun for combat, of course, is a seven shot auto or pump but not everyone has it when he needs it. You have to go to war with what you have in the inventory, not what so-and-so, the gun expert, says you should have.

A shotgun, compared to other firearms, has an extremely limited range. This can be bad if you are firing across wide and open fields. However, your need for a shotgun is typically greatest in close quarters and in this sort of situation one of the principal worries is injuring innocent people.

The extreme range of No. 00 buck shot is about 610 yards; that of No. 6 bird shot is about 275 yards. The extreme range of a caliber .22 Long Rifle bullet is about one mile. Those are extreme ranges, not lethal ranges, and yet they give you a proportion regarding the carrying power of the projectiles. Shotguns are particularly well suited to combat in an urban enviroment because their lethal range is not very great.

A shotgun is an intimidating weapon, a fright weapon. Often, the very sight of a shotgun will induce thoughts of surrender in an opponent. The sound of the action of a pump gun being jacked back and forth terrifies some people as much as a machine gun would. This is a great advantage. It

THE SHOTGUN IN COMBAT

may enable you to win an encounter without a shot being fired, which is particularly important if you are a police officer.

Police Use Of The Shotgun

The shotgun is the answer to many firepower problems that the police face. First of all, let's look at the real and basic reason why police are armed with pistols. It is because the pistol is light enough, small enough, and in some cases, concealable enough to be carried constantly without getting in the way. It does lack firepower, stopping power, and versatility. Often, police officers caught in shoot-outs wish for something more powerful. They don't always have it available, however pressing the need.

This is why every police vehicle should have at least one shotgun. It is too much to expect American police to tote a shotgun around as basic armament but the car can carry the burden without discomfort. Indeed, some police departments have experimented with putting a shotgun scabbard on a motorcycle. The firepower is close by when you need it.

If you are a police officer there are certain guidelines which you can follow to maximize your chances of survival in an armed confrontation. These may not be in keeping with the policies of your department but after all, what would you prefer, a disciplinary suspension or an inspector's funeral?

When responding to a robbery in progress call take careful note of any cover available to you as you pull up to the scene. Keep in mind that your car is doubtful cover at best, as many firearms including the shotgun will penetrate a car door. It is better to take cover and wait for the robbers to come out than to go in after them.

It is stupidity to give them any warning: "Police — come out with your hands up." etc. They may come out with hostages or barricade themselves inside with them. Waiting for the robbers outside and waving off passers-by so as to have a clear field of fire is the only rational way to go.

It is very important that you identify the getaway car and be prepared to disable it as soon as the robbers come out. Actually the signal for the opening of the firefight should be the

THE SHOTGUN IN COMBAT

shots directed at the getaway car. One member of the team (if more than one officer responds to the call) should be assigned to shoot up the vehicle first. If the car is standing at the curb a couple of slugs in the engine and some double-ought at the tires should do the job. If there is a driver in the car, he should be shot first because he may be armed. Even if he is unarmed he can facilitate the escape of the others. Shooting him will mean that the rest of the gang will have to move his body from behind the wheel before they can drive away. This gives you a few more seconds to stop them.

The shotgun is often called a "riot gun." Despite this nomenclature, it is of no use in a riot. Of course, this depends on what the definition of "riot" is. What we call riot is a civil disorder in which the rioters are unarmed. This definition is typical of the disorders of the past decade. In such a case the shotgun is less useful than a club. In this connection, one of the neglected aspects of the Chicago riots during the 1968 Democratic convention was the fact that the police used only tear gas and their clubs and nobody was killed. With all of the severe criticism leveled at the police this outstanding fact was lost in the shuffle. The Chicago police could not have done this if they had used shotguns.

Shotguns are not efficient as tear gas projectors. There are better weapons available for that. Their severe firepower is useless in a situation in which the public-relations aspect has to be considered and the demonstrators are unarmed.

Some situations will be encountered in which what starts out as a demonstration or riot becomes an armed affray with shots fired on both sides. Then is when a shotgun can be useful. However, it must be noted that when this happens you have an insurrection or a revolution rather than a riot.

The Shotgun For Home Defense

In the opinion of many the shotgun is the ideal weapon for home defense. This is an opinion that is shared by both those proficient with firearms and those who barely know the basics.

There are many reasons for this preference. Perhaps the most important one is that the shotgun is easy to handle and to use. It is a big weapon but in your own home there is no need for concealment. It is naturally used with both hands, unlike the pistol, and pointing or aiming it is easier than pointing or aiming the pistol. In this regard, keep in mind that at the short ranges found in home defense situations the spread of shot is not very great. Even with a cylindrical bore, as we've seen in our patterning tests, the spread does not exceed four inches at ten feet. In practice you cannot dispose of two intruders with one blast, even if they're standing side by side. Happily, intruders seldom come in pairs.

Because of the last-mentioned fact, even a single shot weapon will do for home defense most of the time. The chances of being invaded by a gang, "Helter Skelter" style, are small, but even then you have a chance with a single shot, although you'd surely feel more comfortable with a pump-action or a .50 caliber Browning on a tripod.

Be that as it may, your chances of survival and protecting your family in a home defense situation depend upon two things; your weapon and your tactics.

Since protecting your family is a prime requirement, you'll naturally be concerned with another of the shotgun's features; penetrating power. You do not want to have your shot go through a wall with enough force to kill innocent people on the other side. The results of our tests, as illustrated in the accompanying photographs, show us several things.

First, interior walls are rather flimsy and almost anything will penetrate them. The only charge that failed to go through our section of interior wall in our tests was No. 8 bird shot at a range of thirty three feet. However, the bird

THE SHOTGUN IN COMBAT

shot had penetrated when fired from ten feet. The difference is due to the poor ballistic coefficient of spherical projectiles. Balls slow down faster in air than do sharp-pointed cylinders. In a home defense action, all that this means is that if you used a rifle a wild shot might go out through a window and carry for hundreds of yards with enough force to kill or injure an innocent person. A pistol shot would, too, but for a shorter overall range. It is impossible to give precise figures because the ballistics vary with the caliber of weapon and the conditions in which it is fired. For example, as stated before, a rifle bullet going out of a window and suffering minimal deformation as a result, might be flattened by the time it came out, and would not carry beyond fifty yards with any force. This would be particularly true if it were a high-speed hollow-point. A flat disc of lead and copper weighing ninety grains and measuring three-quarters of an inch has a worse ballistic coefficient than a lead sphere.

Two other factors enter to further confuse the situation. The intruder may be armed with a gun, and if he is you can take it for granted that he is not overly concerned with protecting innocent people. By implication, it is important to take him out before he can fire, even at some risk to yourself.

The other factor works in your favor. With a shotgun, as with most other firearms, it is possible to shoot through interior walls. This means that the intruder, once inside your house or apartment, has practically no cover. He may not realize this. If an exchange of fire develops he may take "cover" behind a wall or a piece of furniture in the comfortable delusion that this will protect him from your fire. If you know his approximate location you can shoot right through the wall or furniture with an excellent chance of killing or disabling him.

One result of our tests is particularly relevant to the problem of protecting innocents. We found that No. 8 bird shot went through a wall, when fired at ten feet, to penetrate a third piece of wallboard immediately behind it. Number four buck went sailing through a piece of wallboard located twenty feet beyond our section of interior wall. The precise interpretation of this must be very clear. While it would be going too far to claim that penetration of a piece of wallboard is equal to killing or disabling a human opponent, there is no need to take on a hair-splitting definition of precisely what constitutes disabling or stopping power when the problem is inadvertently injuring innocent people. We feel that any projectiles which can penetrate a wall with enough power to go through a piece of wallboard beyond are a danger to anyone beyond that wall.

We did conduct firing tests against odd pieces of furniture. The results were not worth photographing, as most people would admit that a few layers of fabric and some padding do not offer much resistance to any firearms.

Exterior walls are another matter. Brick or block walls will resist almost anything. Wooden walls or those with aluminim siding are less robust, of course, but they still offer greater resistance to penetration than do interior walls.

The case of trailers or mobile homes is a special problem. The walls are in some cases literally made of cardboard, or something close to it. It would not be much of an exaggeration to say that a slingshot or a B-B gun could penetrate some mobile home walls.

PLANNING THE DEFENSE OF YOUR HOME

It should be obvious that home defense should be planned, not improvised when the moment comes. Nevertheless, many householders have successfully defended their homes against intruders because they were intimately familiar with the layout and the intruder wasn't, and the intruder was not very proficient and didn't have an assault plan. Another important factor is motivation: the intruder is not desperately defending his home. He can retreat if the going gets tough, and try another place tomorrow. The householder is with his back to the wall. There is no place to which he can retreat. However, a little planning in advance can be immensely reassuring if and when the moment comes.

There are three elements in a home defense plan: warning, shelter, and fields of fire. The first, warning, can be covered quickly because it is so obvious. You should know

THE SHOTGUN IN COMBAT

who is coming into your home at all times, day or night. Naturally, you find out who is there before you open the door when the bell rings. However, you should have some passive warning systems to alert you if someone tries to get in without ringing the bell, particularly at night. Entrances should be obstructed in an unobtrusive way, as explained in my previous book, "Shoot-out".

In preparing your plan it is important to see the situation as an intruder would. Take a walk around the outside. Look in through every doorway and window. Note carefully the field of view. This is a good beginning towards the next part, shelter.

You may want to find a place where your family will be safe while the action is going on, where they can lay passive until it is safe to come out. We assume here that you are the head of household and have a wife and perhaps children to worry about. If you are living, on the other hand, with your widowed mother and three husky grown-up brothers, it is another situation.

The best place to hide is in the bathroom. The inside is not visible to anyone peering in the windows. If the bathroom has a window it is usually small and frosted. The door has a lock on it, which can be a help. More importantly, the shower enclosure or bathtub offers a high degree of resistance to bullets. Fiberglass or tile are not as flimsy as the typical interior wall. Many bathtubs are made of steel, covered with epoxy or porcelain. This is not really armor plate, but it is better than anything else. Finally, the usual bathroom has only one entrance, and your wife can, if she is also armed, keep it covered and defend herself if you are disabled or killed. This is defense in depth.

The bathroom's ability to protect the occupants against gunfire can be enhanced very easily. While the sink and toilet will deflect bullets, an additional sheet of inch-thick plywood inside the cabinet will make a whole section of wall resistant to most projectiles. Tiling the walls, if they are not already tiled, will help a lot. Sheet steel, if you can get it cheaply and fit it in without it being conspicuous, is the best. A sheet of mild steel only one-quarter of an inch thick will stop a

THE SHOTGUN IN COMBAT

metal-piercing nine millimeter bullet.

Sheet steel sounds like an outlandish way to protect yourself but sometimes it is practical. If you are buying a house and it is not yet completed you have the opportunity to put steel plate in the walls where you want it.

The subject of shelter also includes protection for your firing point. A bulletproof position goes a long way toward ensuring your survival. There are several ways of protecting yourself from gunfire. One is to pick a place that is around a corner from the intruder's likely approach. While an interior wall is hardly bulletproof if fired at point-blank, it is not the same if you fire obliquely. The studs will stop almost anything. If you are around a corner the only way an opponent can shoot at you, except for an exposed part of your body, is to fire obliquely through the wall.

If it is impossible to pick such a position, it may be possible to armor a closet or a piece of furniture. A couple of layers of Kevlar cloth under the covering of a couch will make it impervious to any caliber likely to be encountered. A cabinet can have a piece of plywood or steel inside as a shield.

If all of this is not practical it is not hopeless for you. Most of the time, speed and surprise will work in your favor. If you can shoot the intruder before he is even aware that you are awake, you won't need any armor plate. Your early warning system can make this possible. Moreover, the intruder might be deterred by the noise he makes and decide to abandon the effort.

Choosing fields of fire is the final and perhaps most difficult task. Study each access to your living space. Be aware of each way the intruder might come in. Pick firing positions for each one so that you can see and not be seen. Note if there is any cover or concealment nearby for the intruder. Be aware of what is behind him, so that if you miss you know where your shots go. Try to fire upward to avoid inadvertently shooting into a neighbor's window.

In most states the intruder must be in your house or apartment before you can legally shoot him. Keep this in mind when planning your defense. You can't usually shoot

THE SHOTGUN IN COMBAT

someone while he's still trying to pick the lock on your door. In such a case it is wiser to use the time to call the police. However, sometimes the law can and should be ignored. Survival is the first rule. If, for example, there are multiple intruders and you are engaged in a firefight, you should not hesitate to shoot if you get a clear shot at one through a window. The lawyers can try to disentangle the legal niceties later on, but paying a lawyer is better than paying an undertaker.

The field of fire you select will depend on the access route the intruder chooses. It will depend on the size and layout of your living space. It will also depend upon your personality. You may decide to meet the intruder as soon as he sets foot into your house and shoot him then. You may decide that you'll simplify the problem by giving him the run of the house and only defending the bedroom and the bathroom, letting him carry out whatever he chooses from the other rooms.

If you choose the more agressive course of action you will have to select a firing point and field of fire for every possible mode of ingress. You may have to compromise. You may not be able to have each firing point equally armored for your protection.

WHEN THE MOMENT COMES

You are most likely to be awakened by a sound, that of the intruder knocking something over or stumbling heavily. Hopefully, you will be able to come awake fast enough to be effective. If there is time, your wife will go into the bathroom with her pistol or gather the children up and get them to safety. It might be best for them to drop out of a bedroom window and go to a neighbor's house and call the police. All of this takes time and makes noise, however.

You reach under the bed for your shotgun, which should be fully loaded. You may choose to keep one in the chamber and the safety on, or you may want to keep the action open and the chamber empty. Whatever the case, be consistent. You don't want to be fumbling with a gun when you're half

THE SHOTGUN IN COMBAT

awake with an enemy in the house. If you have children keeping a loaded gun around is an additional problem. You may have to keep it locked up during the day and only take it out when you prepare for bed. If you have a single shot weapon, you should have a few spare rounds nearby.

What do you put into the gun, anyway? Will your choice be rifled slugs, No. 4 buck, or what? There is a lot of room for controversy here. The fact is that at point-blank range, say ten feet, anything will make a serious, if not fatal, wound. The critical factor seems to be carrying power. The smaller the shot size, the less it will travel with killing force. This is important in a built-up neighborhood but out in the toolies it is of little importance. For most people buckshot is the answer. Anything from No. 00 to No. 4 will do the job adequately and yet not have so much penetrating power that it poses a danger to the people next door.

Considering the flimsiness of interior walls it is very important for you to know the position of every member of your family before you open fire.

Don't be too anxious to shoot. Try to be sure of the number of intruders you're facing. If you wait any additional ones may reveal themselves to you.

If you suddenly come awake and find that the intruder is in your bedroom with you, play possum. Pretend you're still asleep. Our scenarios have shown us that it is impossible to get to the weapon before he charges and is on top of you. Only if you slept with the weapon in your hand would you have a decent chance of bringing him down before he could get to you and even then it would be a very close thing at best.

You may, if you have the drop on the intruder, call out for him to surrender. This may or may not be a wise course of action. If the intruder is just a kid, you may be impelled by humanitarian motives to do everything you can to spare his life. Keep in mind that by calling out you reveal your position and that he might shoot at you. Worse, he might have accomplices. This could develop into a serious situation for you. Our concensus is — "When in doubt — shoot it out."

THE SHOTGUN IN COMBAT

If you decide to try to persuade the intruder to surrender don't tell him to put up his hands. Tell him to freeze. Do not break cover. On the contrary keep him covered and tell him to turn away from you if he is facing you. Tell him to strip. If you try to frisk him for weapons and all you have is an unwiedly weapon such as a shotgun the chances are that he can grapple with you for it and he might even succeed in taking it away from you. If, on the other hand, you keep your distance and have him take his clothes off, you can satisfy yourself that he has no weapons without risk to yourself.

It is of critical importance that you ascertain the number of intruders before you open fire, if possible. Because of the danger to your family you do want to avoid a firefight. Ideally, you should be able to put them all down before they can return your fire. This might not be possible. They might even get you. That is why it is important for your wife to be armed. Even a .22 pistol will go a long way if she knows how to use it. At the very least she can hold off the intruders until the neighbors, if there are any, have been awakened by the gunfire and called the police, unless you live in New York where everybody minds his own business.

It may happen that the intruders will try to get in several ways. If you are being "Helter Skeltered" you can expect this as a matter of course. At least they will be watching more than one side of the premises. Then it is a matter of both of you taking up defensive positions and shooting it out. If this happens then noise is not important. One of you should get on the phone and call for help if the phone is still working.

If there are two of you with guns your chances of surval, even in a really bad situation, are very much enhanced. You can watch each other's back. You can catch the intruders in a crossfire if the layout permits this. One can cover while the other reloads or changes position. Working together pays off best when you have planned and rehearsed together in advance.

ROOM COMBAT WITH A SHOTGUN

Whether you are the attacker or the defender in a firefight inside a building, having a shotgun gives you a significant

THE SHOTGUN IN COMBAT

advantage. Given the flimsy construction of most interior walls, most firearms will shoot through them, but a shotgun firing slugs can penetrate several walls and still have a lot of power left over. The shotgun with slugs will penetrate most items of furniture found in a home or office, negating their value as cover for your opponent if he tries to use them.

If you are in a situation in which you have to enter a room occupied by an armed opponent, or have to flush one out of a room, the shotgun will make your task easier. The cardinal rule in such a situation is: Don't go in but rather flush him out with firepower. There are several ways to do this with a shotgun. One is to fire a pattern through the wall using slugs until you get him. Another is to fire buckshot through a window or any other aperture, trying to cover the entire room. As the shotgun is not a pinpoint weapon you do not have to be very accurate in your aim. Firing through a window into a room, using the exterior wall for cover and raising only your hands above the level of the sill will work. You can point rather than aim the weapon with devastating effect.

If you must go into a room do not try to kick the door in, as the cops do on TV. Most doors have about as much resistance to bullets as a sheet of cardboard and if he chooses to shoot at the moment that you're standing in front of the door it will be your body that will stop the bullets, not the door. The alternative is to blow the door away with a few shotgun blasts. Exactly how many you'll need depends on the construction of the door and what you're firing. Number four buck is a good choice for shattering a door. The twenty-seven pellets do a lot of damage. The sight of several charges of number four coming through the door may so demoralize the occupant of the room that he might surrender immediately.

If he does not you now have an aperture through which to fire several more blasts if the first ones through the door have not gotten him. You can sweep the room with your shotgun and if you have a partner to assist you, you can, from each side of the doorway, start at the corners and meet in the center. Don't overlook the possibility that he might be behind the door. Fire a couple of blasts through the wall next to the door to eliminate that possibility.

If the defender has somehow managed to survive all this then you may have to go in and get him. Diving into the room is safer if you have a partner with a shotgun covering you. While your partner fires into the room to keep the defender's head down, dive in and head for the floor. Keep in mind that you might not want to take the shotgun with you, as it is awkward to manipulate while lying on the floor. The weapon of choice here is a pistol.

Once you are in wait for the defender to make the first move. Do not give away your position by moving or making any noise. Let your partner make all the noise he wishes by firing into the corners of the room. You should have the defender outflanked and be able to nail him as he ducks for cover, fires back, or tries to flee.

DEFENDING YOURSELF IN A ROOM WITH A SHOTGUN

The first thing you should do when entering a room in which you expect to be assaulted is to look for the exit or exits. It may become necessary to leave in a hurry. Always keep in mind, during the course of the firefight, how many of the enemy there are and where are they. Theoretically, a raiding party should have all of the exits covered but sometimes they slip up or are short of manpower. Be prepared to take advantage of any gap in their preparations.

The next thing is to arrange some cover for yourself. Most furniture is as flimsy as the walls are and offers little protection from gunfire. Nevertheless you can pile some furniture together for more protection than the individual pieces would offer. At the very least try for some concealment. If you have the time, place the lighter pieces of furniture next to the doors and windows to obstruct the assailants if they try to crash in on you. The lighter pieces will trip them up and generally impede them without giving them any cover.

Whatever position you choose, try to arrange it so that you can cover all the entries. If this is not possible, park

THE SHOTGUN IN COMBAT

yourself in front of the one which is least likely to be used by the assailants, for example, the door leading to the bathroom in a hotel room, or a window ten stories off the ground.

If the adjoining rooms are accessible to you, the best course of action is to defend that room by fire from the adjoining one. That way you are already out of the likely line of fire and you force the enemy to cross an open space to get to you. In fact, if one or more of them does manage to break in, they will be hesitant and disorientated at not finding you immediately in front of them and this will give you a moment's edge in the ensuing shoot-out.

It will be to your advantage to start the shooting yourself once you are convinced that the people outside mean you harm and know that you are in there. You can guess how many there are and their approximate positions from their voices, if you can hear them. In any event, putting a rifled slug through the wall on each side of the doorway will probably get one or more of them. Don't forget to put one through the door, too. There might be one standing in front of it listening.

Be always alert to the need for escape and the possibilities of doing so. If they are all clustered in front you might get out of a back door or window after the initial burst of fire, while they are sorting out their casualties and getting reorganized. Alternately, if there is a party covering the back, you might manage to eliminate the ones in front and run boldly out the front door.

A Sample Plan For Home Defense

Diagram "A" illustrates a typical house plan. The heavy lines, the exterior walls, can be considered more or less impervious to gunfire. The interior walls, which show as finer lines, are the usual stud and board construction and are robust enough to stop a BB gun, but nothing else.

Almost all houses have at least one room which does not have an exterior wall nor, of course, a window. In this example Bath 2 is such a room. In addition, it has a bathtub instead of a shower, and we have the option of reinforcing the walls further. In this hypothetical example, we have half-inch mild steel plate in the walls of the bathroom up to chest level. This provides a good refuge for the wife and children. They go in there at the first sign of trouble, the wife armed with a handgun or whatever she can fire well.

Another feature of that second bathroom is its central location. If need be, the occupants can flee through several rooms of their choice. As it is highly unlikely that intruders will surround the house and cover all of the exits, a contingency plan should be made covering the need for a quick exit.

The entire shaded area is known as the "defensive core." This is the functional center of the house. From it, you can cover all of the entries but two with gunfire. Ideally, you should be able to cover them all, but nothing is perfect in this life and you will have to make do with a less than ideal defensive position unless you have a house custom-built along the lines of a bunker.

The two entries which you cannot cover directly are the window of Bath 1 and the two doors of the utility room. Note, however, that if the intruder comes in the window of Bath 1, he can only go on into the bathroom without exposing himself to your fire. Also, if he comes in the outer door to the utility room, he stays bottled up in there unless he comes into the family room, where he will be well within your sight. Staying in the utility room will not protect him, though. You can fire through the wall and finish him in there.

THE SHOTGUN IN COMBAT

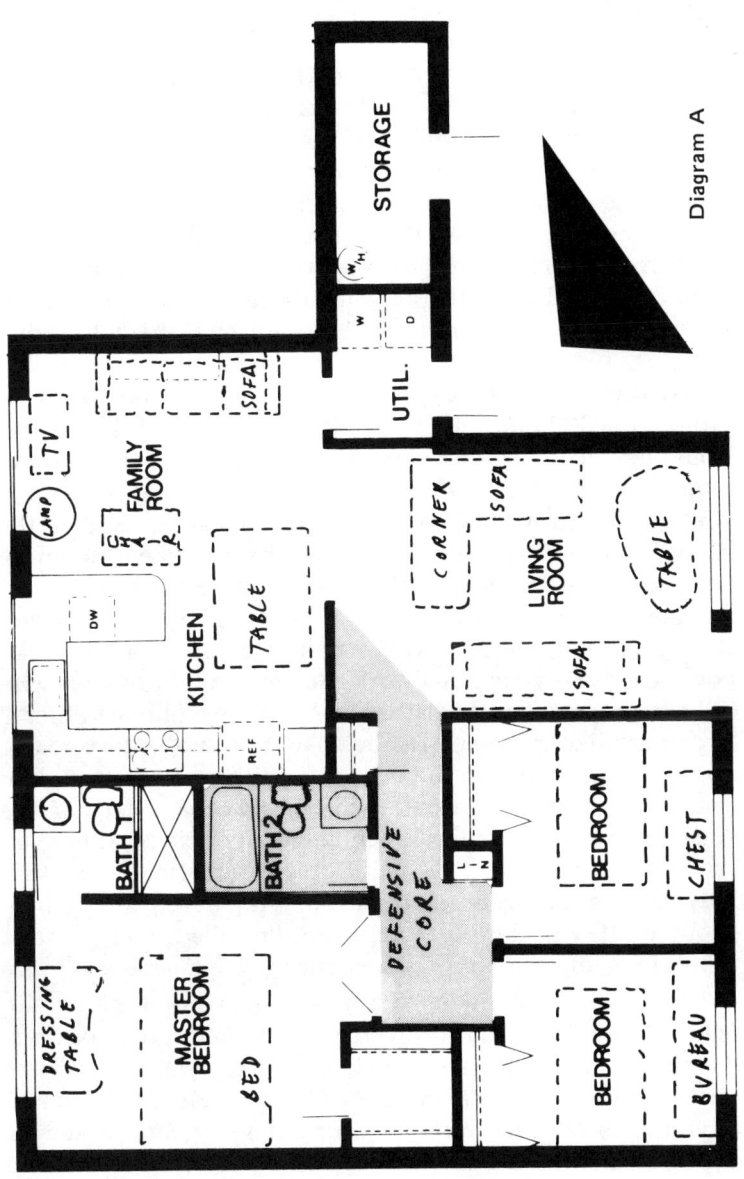

THE SHOTGUN IN COMBAT

Of course, the house should have enough outside lighting and it should be turned on at night. That will silhouette any intruder as he is coming in.

You will note that all of the entries are obstructed or protected by locks. The doors all have tumbler locks and the windows all have some piece of furniture in front of them to impede easy access. This all contributes to your margin of security. Your first warning that someone is trying to get into your home, if you do not own a pet, may well be the noise of his forced entry. It is possible to break a door down in seconds but picking the lock takes time and often makes some noise. So does forcing a window, even if it is only a dull thud.

At the first warning, you get your shotgun and your wife gathers the kids up, quietly we hope, and goes into Bath 2. You take up a defensive position in the shaded area and cover the room from which you heard the noise. Naturally, you do not turn the lights on or do anything to alert the intruder. You wait to see from where he is coming and, more importantly, whether he is alone or has some buddies.

Your success will depend not only upon how well you can keep calm in the next few minutes but upon how well you have done your homework. For example, can your wife call the police from the bathroom? Is there a phone in there? If you are like most people the answer is "no". Most people do not have a phone in the bathroom, although a better place for it can hardly be found. It seems to be a fact of the 20th Century life that the phone always rings when you are in the bathroom and many people sometimes wish that they had an extension in there but they never do anything about it. If you decide to have one installed, you'll find it useful for more than calling the police in an emergency.

Another bit of homework you should not neglect: the fields of fire from your protected positions and the positions themselves. A few bits of steel or plywood in the walls at certain corners will deflect a lot of bullets that may be aimed at you. The few walls around your defensive core should be armored. You should also have arranged the furniture in the various rooms so as to give an intruder no cover at all and minimal concealment.

THE SHOTGUN IN COMBAT

It is instructive at this point to review the meaning of the words "cover" and "concealment." "Cover" means protection from observation and gunfire. "Concealment" means protection from observation. It is preferable to deny an intruder either of them, but especially cover. This usually is not a problem, as most furniture built today is lightly built so as to be porous to gunfire but unless it is of the Danish type or a similar style it may offer him some concealment.

Another point to consider in the selection of your firing positions is that you should not fire in the direction of your family if possible, particularly if they do not have the protection of reinforced walls to deflect the bullets.

When you open fire, you should be careful to choose your moment so that any shot which misses the intruder will hit only an outside wall, unless you are using the lighter shot, such as No. 6 birdshot or smaller. You do not want your shot to travel through a window and perhaps injure a neighbor. If there is some distance between your house and the nearest neighbor so much the better. There will be a deep cushion of air to slow down the shot pellets before they hit your neighbor's house.

In this particular plan, some additional protection for you might be had by armoring the near side of the sofa in the living room. The side nearest the defensive core might have some ballistic cloth under the covering fabric, or perhaps some plywood, or even steel plate if you do not care about the weight. Your wife might complain when she moves it to dust underneath, though.

It is particularly important to be flexible and not to be chained to one particular defensive plan. If the intruder gives you a lot of warning before he is actually in the house with you then you might prefer to evacuate your family first. If, for example, you hear the sounds of the outside utility room door being forced, the family might drop out of any of the bedroom windows. Another possibility is that your wife might put the kids in the bathroom but stay herself in the bedroom to phone the police if there is an extension in the bedroom. This is not a particularly hazardous plan as any intruder would have to get through you to get at her.

THE SHOTGUN IN COMBAT

These plans should be discussed in advance so that everyone understands the situation if and when it comes. That will ensure adequate coordination and minimal fumbling. Most importantly, it should be settled in advance who is to make the decisions and give the orders when the time comes. A ship can have only one captain and a home defense situation cannot be ruled by voting or debate when the emergecy strikes. Most likely, you will find that your wife will be happy to let you make the snap decisions. Despite women's lib, women are still content to let the men do the fighting and you should encounter little difficulty in establishing your authority.

The Conditioned Reflex

Many people, when they hear the term "conditioned reflex," think either of Pavlov's dogs salivating at the ring of a bell or of a notorious Communist brainwashing technique. Actually the conditioned reflex is a simple and ordinary thing that we use every day. Many actions that we say that we perform "subconsciously" are those we perform by conditioned reflex.

There are two types of reflexes that belong to this discussion. One is the inborn, or instinctive reflex, which is built into our nervous system and does not need to be learned. For example, if your hand touches a red-hot object, you immediately pull it back without thinking about it. You may jump at a loud noise. This is the startle reflex. You put your arm out to catch yourself if you trip. All of these are inborn reflexes.

The conditioned reflex is a learned action that becomes automatic, so that we perform it without conscious planning of every move. Walking or driving a car are two good examples.

Relfexes can work for us or against us. In shooting, flinching is a result of the startle reflex. The loud noise still causes us to have a startle reflex, even though we have learned not to be frightened by it. We tend to anticipate it and jerk the trigger and even tighten our muscles to brace ourselves against the noise and recoil. We deal with this in two ways, one by wearing ear protection so as to lessen the intensity of the noise, and also by a lot of practice to train ourselves to pull the trigger smoothly. We try to "extinguish" the reflex because it impedes us.

We can also use reflexes for helping us in our shooting. After a certain amount of practice, certain moves become automatic. If there is a safety strap on our holster, we learn to release it without thinking when we draw. We learn to reload the weapon automatically.

Conditioned reflexes vary in complexity. They can be simple, as firing a gun. They can be somewhat more complex,

THE SHOTGUN IN COMBAT

such as drawing, firing, and reloading. They can be very complex indeed, for example, drawing, deciding which target to hit first, and then doing so. This can be important if faced with multiple opponents, such as the classic example of a man with a shotgun, a man with a pistol, and a man with a knife. In such a case fast decision and fast action are essential, and meditating about the proper course of action will get you killed.

Careful training is the answer. Building up those conditioned reflexes so that the time you waste is minimal will speed up your reactions in combat. The more of the proper conditioned reflexes you can build up the more you will free your mind to make the decisions that cannot be made in advance.

It helps to standardize your moves and practice them often. If you carry your pistol in a holster with the strap snapped, always keep it snapped, for the sake of consistency and to reduce fumbling when you draw. If you carry your shotgun with the breech empty, the magazine full, and the slide back, always carry it that way. For the sake of building up conditioned reflexes and making them work for you it is more important to be consistent than to be correct.

What this means is that it is better to practice something and learn it well than it is to abide by a procedure labelled as "correct" but not practice it so that is becomes automatic. For example, if you are a policeman carrying a pistol and your department requires that the holster be snapped at all times, then practice drawing from this condition, even though it is better for the sake of a fast draw to start from an open holster. The difference in speed between the two is not very much, far less than the difference between someone who practices from an unsnapped holster when you're out shooting on your own time. You'll build up a conditioned reflex that will impede you in the long run. If ever you get into a shootout and you're used to drawing from an unsnapped holster, but this time it is snapped, you may lose several seconds or even drop the gun in your efforts to free it.

If you're used to carrying the shotgun with the magazine loaded, breech empty, and the slide back, you will only cross

THE SHOTGUN IN COMBAT

yourself up if you one day decide to carry it with one up the spout and the safety on. If you decide to change your method of carry, practice getting your weapon into action the new way, so that the old conditioned reflex becomes extinguished and the new one takes its place.

It is of the utmost importance to be consistent. You cannot do one thing in practice and another when the real thing comes along. One conspicuous example is picking up shells. If you reload you naturally are concerned with saving your empties and reusing them. You may even have built up the habit of taking your eyes off the target after each shot to see where your shell has dropped, or picking it up. In combat, this can get you killed. At the very least it distracts you from your main task, that of staying alive. It can lose you time. It can expose you to enemy fire, if you break cover to pick up a shell.

It pays to minutely dissect your every move in practice and to ask yourself if you'd do this in the real thing. If the answer is no, then practice better habits.

Never forget that the habits you develop in practice will stay with you in combat. If you are serious about developing your combat skills think of this often. It is a point so obvious and so fundamental that it is often overlooked or ignored. The conditioned reflexes that you build up in time of peace are those with which you will go to war.

Preparing For Combat

Gunfights happen fast. The typical encounter is settled within a few seconds and the opponents do not even get to empty their guns. The element of surprise is usually present and there is no time to plan the moves. If you make a mistake, you do not get the luxury of going back and doing it over. You must be quick and accurate, or you will be dead.

There are not many experienced gunfighters around. It is a very deadly sport and few survive to tell of their experiences. How, then, do you learn to be competent in a gunfight, if there are few competent teachers around and you are not likely to live to learn from experience? One method is to practice using scenarios, as outlined in a later chapter.

Practice is important. In a real shoot-out, you are not likely to have the time either to plan your moves or to try again if you make a mistake. You must have mastered the basic moves already so that when you have to, you will make the right moves by conditioned reflex rather than by conscious deliberation. It cannot be repeated too often: in a gunfight you do not have the time to think it out.

The basic moves include, but are not limited to: drawing your weapon, firing accurately under pressure, reloading, clearing jams, taking cover instantly instead of looking around to see what is causing the commotion, and using preplanned strategies. It goes without saying that you should be familiar with your weapon and its use so that you can use it, reload it, and clear any jams without deliberating over it. This should be automatic, like walking or driving a car. After enough practice, also known as conditioning, you will be able to do so. However, it is important to practice the right moves, to build up the correct habits. If you are used to standing up to reload, or if you pick up your brass as you fire, your career in a real shootout will be very short and you will be able to measure your life expectancy with a stopwatch. In practicing you must at all times act as if there is someone out there shooting at you.

Taking cover is instinctive. Nevertheless it must be practiced. Imagine what would happen if you suddenly are fired

THE SHOTGUN IN COMBAT

at and the only cover close enough is a gutter full of water or mud. If you hestitate while telling yourself that getting your clothes dirty is better than getting shot, you may give your opponent enough time to get a hit on you.

You may have a cup of hot coffee in your hand. If you take the time to put it down neatly on the table, without spilling a drop, before going for your weapon, the blood spilling may be yours.

Using pre-planned strategies is the most difficult part. In a shoot-out you cannot plan in detail unless you have the initiative, such as in a stakeout or an ambush. Normally you are forced to react and you must be prepared to do so. As you cannot foresee every possible situation you must construct your strategy on the spot from pre-planned building blocks, canned plans if you will, that permit you to tailor your response as the situation demands. This means that you must already know the answers to various questions that will face you on the spot. For example, at what range will you try to return fire immediately and when do you go for cover first? If ambushed, do you charge the enemy or duck for cover while you look for an escape route? Is the primary objective to kill or capture your opponent? What about innocent bystanders?

The answers to these questions depend in part upon your knowledge of your own abilities. You should know, for example, at what range you can draw and fire from the hip and be assured of getting a hit with the first shot or two. You should know what is the maximum range at which you can hit a man with your weapon. Note the emphasis on the word "you." It does you no good to be told that a certain gun expert can hit a beer can at a hundred yards with a pistol, unless he is going to accompany you on your next shoot-out. It's what *you* can do that counts. You also should know the basic capabilities of your weapon. It is very helpful to know, if you have a shotgun loaded with slugs, that you can fire right through an interior wall of a house and nail the enemy taking cover behind it. It helps to know that if you are faced with two gunmen forty yards away, whether you can hit them both with one pattern of double-ought.

THE SHOTGUN IN COMBAT

If you practice scenarios of the various situations you expect to face you will get most of the answers that you need. You can experiment with various solutions that occur to you, and if you get in a tight spot you can apply the knowledge and experience gained from your practice. More importantly, you'll be able to make the life-and-death decisions quickly, without wasting time.

THE SCENARIO METHOD

The "scenario" method is the key to developing effective tactics and techniques for combat shooting. Most of us have not ever been in a gunfight and since a certain proportion of those who are do not survive to learn from their experiences, another method is needed to test and clarify gunfighting tactics.

The dictionary defines "scenario" as meaning a plot outline, a theme. For our purposes, this is excellent. The basic method is to construct a scenario of a shoot-out and then try it on for size, as it were, to determine how it works out in practice.

The first step is to outline a situation in which you would have to use firepower to resolve the problem. It is not necessary to totally invent the situation. Many sources of real shoot-outs are available, for example: police reports, newspaper accounts, books and magazines. Indeed, one excellent way to start is to restage a shoot-out that already happened to see if you can make any improvement on the tactics used. It is usually easy to do some "Monday morning quarterbacking" on this type of situation, because in a real shoot-out people make decisions hurriedly and under stress and this leads to many errors.

Some books which have valid accounts of shoot-outs are the following:

"Target Blue" — Robert Dailey
"Combat Shooting for Police" — Paul Weston
"Fort Apache" — Tom Walker

The key word here is "valid." Fictional accounts are not reliable, as often they are written by novelists who know

THE SHOTGUN IN COMBAT

nothing about guns and shooting and who make such blunders as having their heroes slipping off the safety catch on their revolvers or using a silencer which makes the report sound like a whisper. Some fiction writers seem to believe that the impact of a .45 caliber bullet will pick the victim up and throw him ten feet. It is difficult enough to construct a scenario which is rigorously accurate without being handicapped by a fiction writer's fantasies.

Alternately, you can imagine a situation in which you might be involved but which hasn't yet happened, such as facing an intruder in your home or a stickup where you work. In that case you'd have the imcomparable advantage of being on the scene and of looking over the actual "terrain" on which the incident might occur.

Once you've selected a situation, work out a probable course of action for your opponents and plan of action for yourself. You should include the following factors, at least: time, place, weapons used, positions of antagonists, availability of cover, your opponent's purpose and plan, your countermoves, etc.

There are many factors which may or may not apply, depending on the situation. Some of them are: availability of help or reinforcements, visibility if it takes place at night, innocent bystanders, hostages, but these factors must be applied realisitically, as you cannot have either side doing anything that they would not be likely to do in real life.

Once you've determined the setting and the scenario you're ready to act it out. It is best to do a dry run first, with empty guns. This enables you to have a live opponent without danger. You might find that some features of your plan are unworkable, for example, in a home defense situation you might find that slipping the safety off your weapon makes too much noise and alerts the intruder to your presence. You might find, too, that a shotgun's size imposes some restrictions on your movement, such as in getting out of a car quickly and quietly.

Next comes a run-through with live ammunition. Unlike the dry run, you cannot conduct this in your home or wherever you want. You'll have to do it out in the boonies or somewhere else safe. You'll also want to use silhouette targets to represent your opponent or opponents. Paper or cardboard silhouettes are desirable for several reasons. They are light and cheap. They can be easily carried and put up. They show the exact placement of hits, as compared with steel targets. They also show clearly the holes from different weapons or calibers, which is important if you are using two or more weapons if you are working with a partner. You might be armed with a shotgun and your partner with a pistol. Then you will want to see who got the hits, if any.

Between the dry run and live firing, you'll get a chance to observe and work out kinks in your scenario. Some element of the plan turns out to be unworkable or the enemy's reponse has been underestimated. Often, the problem will turn out to be one of timing. A planned course of action takes too long, far too long, enough for your opponent to fire a whole magazine at you, or to escape.

Some examples of unworkable scenarios in our own test are the following:

One scenario which has the shooter turning, drawing and firing two shots at each of three targets with a pistol resulted in too much time elapsing. The underlying assumption was that the shooter would be able to put two bullets into each of the three opponents before they were able to react and get him. In over fifty test runs with several different shooters, this turned out to be unworkable in all but one trial. When a second shooter was designated to represent the third opponent, and to draw, turn, and fire, upon a fourth target as soon as he heard the first shot, it turned out to be impossible except in one freakish instance, for the first shooter to place his shots before the second one was able to respond and hit the fourth target, which for the purposes of the tests represented the first shooter. We ran the tests with both experienced and novice shooters and switched positions and even weapons to simulate varying conditions. We even used shotguns in some trials. This series of trials was a turning point in our experimentation, for it showed that a scenario which many people had accepted as valid had indeed a

THE SHOTGUN IN COMBAT

serious flaw, and it confirmed the need to try everything out, rather than blandly assume that it would work just because some "gun expert" said so.

Another scenario which turned out to have an unworkable feature was one in which three shooters drove by three targets and fired at them while the vehicle was moving. It was pointed out, after several trials in which the targets were riddled, that the vehicle was driven at such a funereal pace and the action took place so slowly that there was more than adequate time for the targets to recover from their surprise and return fire. Again, the plan had to be modified in the light of reality.

Yet another scenario that was not satisfactory was a series of trials of the ability of a sleeping person to respond to an intruder charging him. Fortunately, a trial such as this can be done with an empty weapon, for maximum safety. The scenario was that the defender would be in bed when the intruder opened the bedroom door and charged him. The problem would be to bring the pistol into action soon enough to stop the charge. We found that if the door was assumed to be ten feet or closer, that it was impossible for the defender to pick up the pistol from under the pillow and bring it up in time, before the intruder was upon him, that is, close enough to push the pistol away with one hand and stab or shoot him with the other. It was not necessary to try getting the pistol out of a dresser drawer or from under the mattress, as it was obvious that there was not enough time. The conclusion was obvious: it was essential to be awake and armed, ready to fire, before the intruder arrived at the bedroom door. This led to our devising the "early-warning" set-up, that is, arranging furniture around all the windows so that any intruder would make noise upon entering.

It helps greatly to have a third party along as observer. An observer who is exactly that, who does not participate in the scenario at all, can often spot shortcomings and weaknesses that the participants miss. Many times a shooter will break cover by standing up to reload, or clear a jam. He and the other shooters may not notice this but the observer will, as would the adversary in a real exercise, before breaking cover to go check the targets. This could be a fatal error in real life, but the shooters were unaware of it until the observer pointed it out. Often, the shooters are unaware of how much time is elapsing because they are energetically participating in the action. The observer can count the seconds for a determination of whether that length of time is realistic in that sort of situation.

The scenario is a way to test responses to a situation, to modify them or even to abandon a plan that proves to be unworkable and adopt one that is.

DEVISING YOUR OWN SCENARIOS

1. Try for realism as much as possible.

2. Most real-life combat shooting is done from close-up. Accordingly, keep the ranges short. Avoid the temptation to lengthen the ranges just to add an extra challenge to the exercise. "Close-up" means seven yards or less according to the FBI and most American police officials, four yards or less if you follow Fairbairn and Sykes. Use cardboard targets to prevent ricochets.

3. Don't wast much time with weak-handed shooting. It is best to concentrate on downing your enemy before he gets you. If you assume he's wounded you, you've lost half the battle.

4. Since most shoot-outs take place from very close up have some targets very close — within arm's length. Try shooting the shotgun with one hand in some cases. You will not need to aim, just point the gun.

5. In real life the shoot-out does not begin with the participants standing with their hands clasped, awaiting the start signal. Start in a natural position for the situation.

6. Often shots are fired after a chase or a fight. There should be some scenarios in which the shooter is required to run a certain distance before opening fire, to get the hearbeat and respiration up. Usually in real life the adrenaline is pumping hard. After all, it is a life and death situation.

THE SHOTGUN IN COMBAT

7. Often in real life shots are fired from awkward positions. There should be some situations included in which the shooter is required to fire from an awkward position, such as standing on a ladder or a narrow ledge.

8. Available cover should always be used. There is, in real life, cover of some sort almost anywhere, in urban or rural areas, and the shooter should be encouraged to avail himself of this cover. Do not use the conventional police "barricade" position, which is rarely seen in real life. Rather, use a car door, car hood, table top, etc. Often the cover is inadequate but it still offers some concealment and support for the firearm.

9. Never allow the shooter to reload or clear jams from the standing position. This offers the opposition a still target, and in real life you can't spot the opposition any advantage at all. Insist that the shooter use cover when available or crouch or lie prone when in the open, except for the first shot.

10. Psychological hazards are often present: cup of coffee in the hand, hostages, etc. These should be included as much as possible.

11. There are sometimes situations in which a choice must be made between targets of varying priority, for example a man with a gun at ten yards and a man with a knife at five.

12. Always keep the scenario consistent with events in real life, otherwise it is worse than useless: it is misleading.

Miscellaneous Situations

NIGHT ENCOUNTERS

One moonless night we enacted an ambush scenario, with three targets facing two of us at a distance of about thirty feet. We ran through it a couple of dozen times with increasing consternation for we found, as we re-holstered our pistols after each trial, that we were hardly hitting the targets at all. It became obvious that although the targets were out in the open and not under cover of any sort as human opponents might well be, we were not defending ourselves adequately in that situation. Even with luminous sights we could not see the targets clearly enough in the ambient light to place hits.

We would surely have done better with flashlights but that would have been making brilliant targets of ourselves. In an ambush situation it is of prime importance to return fire as soon as possible, without wasting time fumbling for a flashlight and certainly without giving the enemy a well-lit aiming point. The so-called "cop's trick" of holding the flashlight at arm's length would not work in an ambush because the ambushers would be pouring a storm of fire around every possible target.

One obvious solution to our problem was to use shotguns. A pistol, or any single-projectile weapon, that must be aimed or pointed with some precision is difficult to use if you cannot see your target. However, at thirty feet, the range of the targets in this scenario, the pattern from a cylindrical bore shotgun is about two feet in diameter. This gives a great margin for error. The shotgun at any but the shortest ranges fires a pattern, making it easier to hit a target that you cannot see clearly.

One other outstanding feature of a shotgun used at night is the flash, which seems as bright as an atom bomb. This will advertise your position but hopefully your firepower will make it all academic. The usual caution applies. Make good use of cover, if available, and your problems with enemy fire will be reduced.

THE SHOTGUN IN COMBAT

THE ARMORED OPPONENT

With the proliferation of lightweight ballistic cloth vests, the shotgun becomes more and more attractive as the weapon of choice. Many of these "bulletproof" vests protect the torso against cal. .38 Special bullets and the like, but they do not stand up against the 12 gauge shotgun, if it is properly handled.

A rifled slug will whiz through the "armor" as if it were just a skirt. So will buckshot at short ranges. At longer ranges using buckshot allows you to get hits in the head and the limbs, which are not armored, much more easily than you could with a pistol.

AMBUSHES

It is almost always possible to prepare for an ambush and this means that a preponderance of firepower can usually be had by the ambushing party. With enough time, shotguns can be obtained, as well as any other weapons that may be deemed necessary.

The shotgun, used from a well-protected position, enables you to dominate the scene and to pour a rain of lead into the killing zone.

If you are stopping a car, a slug in the engine will often cripple the vehicle, while a couple of follow-up blasts of double-ought in the windshield will seriously impair the driver's ability to drive, and perhaps to breathe too. Once the car is stopped, a barrage of buckshot will quickly stifle the opposition and restore peace and quiet to the scene.

RIOTS AND PUBLIC DISTURBANCES

The term "Riot Gun" is a misnomer. The shotgun is deadly force and there are few public disorders that justify using it. Most of the time tear gas or clubs will be enough. Some police departments use tear gas shells in shotguns but these have little capacity and are not very effective when

THE SHOTGUN IN COMBAT

compared to the specially designed gas grenade launchers now in vogue.

Only if a riot threatens human life is there any justification for using firepower to stop it. While it may be comforting to the police to have shotguns handy in riot situations there will rarely be any occasion to use them.

IF YOU ARE CAUGHT IN THE OPEN

This situation, like many others, was covered in "Shoot-Out," but a few words about the use of the shotgun are appropriate here.

Being caught in the open may be the result of an ambush or it may be the result of other circumstances, but the exigencies are the same. Without cover, the best defense is a vigorous offense. The shotgun, particularly the multi-shot pump or auto type, is capable of delivering a heavy barrage of fire for those critical few seconds that you will need to reach cover or to permit your companions to reach cover. This is one of the few situations that so-called "suppressive fire" is justified because of the desperate nature of the situation.

If you can find even light cover, such as a curb or a patch of dead ground, you will be much better off and will be able to make better use of your limited supply of ammunition. Spraying indiscriminately, in the panic of imminent death, leads mainly to the waste of ammo. Still, it may be your only choice.

SHOOTING FROM A CAR

The most obvious fact about using a shotgun from a car is that the shotgun is very unwieldy. It gets tangled up in your legs, seat belt, etc. and is very awkward to manipulate. Because of the bouncing around of the vehicle it is best, for safety's sake, to carry the gun with the chamber empty. Relying on a mechanical safety is a dangerous practice in these circumstances.

Deploying the shotgun and firing from a moving vehicle is easier if the vehicle is open, as is a convertible or if you are in

THE SHOTGUN IN COMBAT

the back of a pickup truck. At least there is room to swing, so to speak.

Firing a shoulder weapon from a moving vehicle poses problems because both firing hands are occupied holding the weapon. You cannot steady yourself with one hand, as you can with a pistol. Here is one instance in which the spreading pattern of the shotgun will work very much to your advantage.

If you are firing at a pursuing vehicle you are in a splendid position. Nothing discourages the driver of the following car so much as a load of double-ought crashing in through his windshield.

WORKING WITH A PARTNER

In some fortunate situations you'll be working with a partner in whom you can have confidence and whose judgment you trust. This gives you an immeasurable advantage over working alone. Your fighting power, according to Lanchester's law, is squared, not merely doubled. You have the advantage of both fire and maneuver and, with good teamwork, you should be able to plan and put into practice moves that you will have worked out beforehand.

It is important to have a partner whom you like and with whom you are intellectually and emotionally compatible. As your relationship develops you will learn each other's way of thinking and be able to predict each other's probable reaction in a given situation. Good teamwork requires planning for various eventualities, and if you are really interested in being well-coordinated, rehearsing the various plans that you draw up. You will find, during these rehearsals, that working with a partner in life and death situations brings a special responsibility. You will learn to literally look out for each other.

Planning is important. While it is impossible to plan what you will do in every conceivable set of circumstances, it is nevertheless possible to plan not only general guidelines for action but certain set responses for various critical situations. While it is true that some situations will take you by surprise,

THE SHOTGUN IN COMBAT

if you have certain "building blocks" of tactics you can improvise the rest on the spot. Some guidelines are:

Try to split up, spread out, and outflank the enemy. Catch him or them in a crossfire if you can.

Stay out of each other's line of fire. Conversely, try to maneuver so that your opponent does not push one of you into the other's line of fire. Moreover, try to maneuver so that one of your adversaries is blocking the other's line of fire.

While splitting up forces so your adversary has to divide his attention, don't split up so far that you lose contact with each other unless you are carrying out a previously agreed-upon plan.

Use the basic infantry tactics of fire and maneuver. One of you gives covering fire to force your enemy to keep his head down while the other changes his position. This is very important. Maneuvering is as important as firepower. You may want to outflank the enemy, or go to get another weapon, go to get help, etc.

Plan certain things in advance. For example, each of the partners should, when opening fire, direct his fire to the adversary or adversaries on his side first. If there are three of them and two of you, and you are on your partner's right, you should open fire on the right-hand one first, then the center one, and finally the left-hand one if your partner has not yet taken him out.

If you are riding in a vehicle and the plan is, if ambushed, to bail out of the vehicle and counterattack, preplan the exit sequence. It won't do to be collidng in the doorway while the ambushers are pouring it in on you. Decide in advance who will cover which side so that there is no confusion when you get outside.

If you are in a house or in a room, decide in advance which side you will each defend.

Be aware, during the firefight, of your partner's status. If you are firing upon several opponents, you may find that your partner has ceased firing because of a jam, or being out of ammo, or some other reason. You must be prepared to take up the slack. If your partner cannot take out the targets

THE SHOTGUN IN COMBAT

on his side you must be prepared to do it for him after you've finished off yours. You must both learn to anticipate each other's moves. For example, you might be aware that your partner's cover is not as good as yours. In that case you should lay down some covering fire to give him a chance to change his position. Reciprocally, he should be prepared to do the same for you.

Try, during your rehearsals together, to develop an awareness of each other's cadence and timing. You should know how long the other takes to reload, how fast the other can run from point A to point B, etc. Timing is all-important in a shoot-out and synchronizing with a partner often makes the difference between life and death.

You should try for a commonality of weapons. This does not mean that you should both carry identical guns but that they should be the same caliber and type. For example, you might both agree to carry Smith&Wesson 9mm automatics and 12 gauge pump action shotguns. This simplifies the ammunition supply problem. It would be extremely awkward if, during a firefight, one of you ran back to the car under fire to get another box of 12 gauge slugs and found out, upon returning to his position of cover, that he was holding a box of 16's.

Be familiar with the other's weapon or weapons. The guns may use the same ammunition but be of different models or makes. In certain circumstances, such as being wounded, it may be important for the other to be able to use the wounded one's weapon, particularly if his own is jammed or otherwise unserviceable.

Since we are a motorized society, a lot of our time is spent in and around cars. If you are working with a partner in a vehicle you should have your planning worked out to even seemingly minor details as who carries what weapons when. The driver obviously cannot drive while holding a shotgun. Whoever is beside him will obviously be the one to "ride shotgun." Does that mean that the driver should have only a pistol or should he keep a shotgun under the seat in the back? If you have to bail out, should the driver stop the vehicle and both of you bail out, or should he slow down to

THE SHOTGUN IN COMBAT

let the shotgunner off and then proceed a few more yards before bailing out himself? How much ammo do you carry on you and how much reserve ammo do you carry in the vehicle? These are some of the questions that must be answered before you will be a well-integrated team.

One of the quickest ways to work out some of your basic tactics is to run through some scenarios together to see how well your basic plans stand up in action. Then, when you have worked out most of the bugs, practice. Practice some more. Then go on to more difficult problems that you cannot handle. There is too such a word as impossible. That way you will learn your strong points and your limitations as a team.

Selected Shotgun Scenarios

The Ambush

Set-up   Several silhouette targets on one or both sides of a road. Two or more shooters in a vehicle to drive down the road. One observer as passenger in the vehicle. Observer may get out between shoots to shift targets around for surprise effect.

Scenario: You are driving along a road when you are ambushed. The signal for the ambush is the observer's shout. Plan a method of dealing with the ambushers, before the action starts, and then carry it out. Decide in advance how to safely carry weapons in the vehicle and who will do what when the action starts.

Critique: After each run talk over your performance. Did you return fire effectively? Did you react quickly enough? Were there any awkward pauses in your response because one person did not know his job or what the other one was doing? Did you use cover effectively? Finally, is the best response to that ambush to stop and shoot it out, or try to drive through it? Why? (hint: roadblocks)

The Ambush, Variation One

Set Up: Same as before but this time from a different vehicle, say a truck or a camper. The driver is restricted to using a pistol, while the passenger(s) may use a shotgun. At the signal, use your weapons appropriately. Try driving through the ambush and see if you can neutralize the ambushers from the moving vehicle, without stopping.

Critique: Which weapon is more effective, pistol or shotgun? Did you feel that you should have stopped and shot it out on the spot?

The Ambush, Variation Two

Set-up: Same as before but this time the passenger(s) "riding shotgun" pile out and shoot it out. So does the driver, if he chooses.

THE SHOTGUN IN COMBAT

Critique: Is your response time faster or slower? Is there anything to be gained by spraying the area?

The Ambush, Variation Three

Set-up: Same as before, but at night. Pistols first, then shotguns.

Critique: Is a shotgun more effective when the targets are hard to see?

Running out of Ammo

Set-up: Five silhouettes at various ranges. Hand shooter a shotgun that does not have enough shells in it to finish the course of fire. Shooter does not know when he'll run out.

Scenario: You are running out of ammo. When the gun goes dry, draw your backup pistol and finish the course of fire with it.

Critique: Was much time lost in changing weapons? Did shooter take cover or at least crouch to make himself a smaller target while drawing his pistol?

Hostage — Decision Making

Set-up: Three silhouettes, two of which are set up with one partially obstructing the other, as in a hostage situation. Shooter has shotgun loaded with rifled slugs. Another shooter has rifle, pistol, or shotgun loaded with slugs. Both shooters are behind cover.

Scenario: You are police officers confronting two armed robbers who have taken a hostage. Your partner is aiming carefully at the hostage-taker while you are covering the other. The plan is for your partner to shoot the hostage-taker while you, upon the sound of the shot, take out the other one before he can harm the hostage. Your partner may miss, in which case you must switch objectives and take out his target first, then your own. Consequently, you must observe whether your partner scores a hit or not before opening fire.

Critique: How quick are you? Are you close enough to see if it's a hit or a miss?

THE SHOTGUN IN COMBAT

Defense Against Surprise Attack at Night

Set-up: One or more shooters sitting around campfire at night. One observer who sets up the silhouettes at different ranges. Observer signals the start of the attack with a shout and times the event.

Scenario: You are sitting around a campfire. Suddenly you are attacked. The first shots miss and you and your partner (if any) counterattack. Take out the targets, using both fire and maneuver.

Critique: Did you get them all? Did you see them all? Did you find it easier to hit with the shotgun or with the pistol? Did you have enough ammo?

Home Defense

Set-up: Shooter is blindfolded. Observer sets up one or two silhouettes at ranges not to exceed twenty-five feet. It is night. Shooter either lies prone or crouches behind a chair. Observer removes blindfold.

Scenario: You are at home and have been awakened by a noise. You take your shotgun and move toward the noise, lie down or take cover and wait for the intruder or intruders. When you see them take your time and make sure that you hit on the first shot. They don't know that you are waiting for them so you have the advantage of surprise. If you miss, they will return fire and may hit your family.

Chasing Two Suspects

Set-up: Two silhouettes thirty yards apart. Shooter has shotgun and starts one hundred yards from nearest silhouette.

Scenario: You are chasing two suspects. You run after them for a hundred yards and then one of them turns and fires at you. You immediately return fire. As soon as you hit him you run over to him. That is where you are when the second suspect opens fire on you. You fire back at him.

THE SHOTGUN IN COMBAT

Critique: Is it better to crouch down when fired upon or to return fire immediately? Discuss and give reasons why or why not.

Store Holdup

Set-up: Two silhouettes twenty feet apart, with a chair by the nearer one. Shooter starts thirty feet from nearer one.

Scenario: You are a police officer summoned to a robbery in progress call. You run towards the store. Halfway there you see the armed suspect. You fire at him. You run to him and then you see another armed suspect around a corner. You crouch and fire around the corner without exposing yourself any more than necessary.

Critique: When should you jack a shell into the chamber? Can you run safely with a loaded gun? Should you assume a low kneeling position when dealing with the second suspect, or a prone position? Why?

Questions & Answers

Can you really learn about gunfighting from a book?

The answer is yes. This brings up another question: "How well?" The answer to that one depends a lot on you and more particularly on how much effort you are willing to make to practice the skills that you learn. Practice and rehearsal will enable you to meet dangerous situations reflexively, without stopping for a few fatal seconds while you are trying to remember what you read. The psycho-motor skill involved in shooting accurately and quickly cannot be learned from a book. A book can tell you how, but then you have to go out and practice.

Since the shotgun has so much more stopping power than the pistol, should I forget about trying to use a pistol and concentrate on developing my skill with a shotgun?

No. The pistol and the shotgun meet different needs. The pistol is lighter, more portable, and much more concealable. If your prime requirement is concealability, for example, you'd want a pistol. A lot of ink has been wasted in delineating the stopping power or lack of it in various pistols. It is obvious that you sacrifice something for the sake of having a small weapon. It should be equally obvious that no weapon is one hundred per cent effective. Read Fairbairn's "Shooting to Live" for a discussion of cases that the forty five caliber pistol did not stop. Read the April 1979 issue of "Soldier of Fortune" for examples of lack of stopping power of both the AK-47 and M-16 rifles. If you are looking for absolute and guaranteed stopping power, consider getting yourself a flame-thrower or a rocket launcher. Anything smaller is a compromise in some respect.

In your book "Shoot-Out" you say not to shoot by sound alone if you can't see your opponent. Is this still true if you're using a shotgun?

THE SHOTGUN IN COMBAT

Originally, we had run tests using blindfolded subjects trying to hit targets as close as ten feet by sound, using a pistol. The percentage of hits was disappointing. We also ran night firing trials, firing at dark targets that blended in with the background to the point of being almost invisible. The ranges varied in the night firing tests but we did have the advantage of being able to use luminous sights. Nevertheless, we found that one hit in ten shots fired was about par. Since then, our patterning tests with the shotgun have convinced us that the shotgun is the weapon of choice in conditions of poor visibility, as the shot pattern spreads significantly beyond ten feet. In other words, a near miss with a pistol is still a miss: a near miss with a shotgun means that you still hit with part of the pattern.

Will shooting in "combat" matches sharpen my shooting skills?

Certainly. In addition they are a lot of fun. However, don't expect that they'll prepare you for an encounter with a target that shoots back. You'll find that the shooting skills and style that you've developed for winning a "combat" match are of little help in a real life situation. It's best to see these matches for what they really are; recreation and a lot of good clean fun.

I'm a police officer and sometimes I worry about my badge and bright buttons making me a better target at night. How important is this?

You've got good reason to worry. All of the bright and reflective metal you wear makes you a better target. Also, the additional equipment such as whistle, handcuffs, and walkie-talkie shake, rattle, and generally advertise your position to anyone without a hearing defect. You may well wonder why handcuffs have to be chrome plated instead of being finished in black teflon. Sad to say, when enough police officers are killed, something may be done about this. Meanwhile, the police supervisors are more concerned with how their men look at inspection than out where it counts.

THE SHOTGUN IN COMBAT

I'm going to use a pistol as a backup when my primary weapon is a shotgun. Is stock angle as important then?

It is very important all of the time. You may have noticed that some pistols point naturally better than others. This is because they fit your hand better. The critical part of this fit is called the stock angle.

If you point your index finger at someone or something with the rest of the hand closed you'll find that a pencil held in the other fingers forms an angle of thirty to forty degrees from perpendicular to your index finger. The exact angle depends on the exact shape of your hand. This is the ideal stock angle for you. The grip, or stock, should be at this angle to the barrel. If so, you'll find that the pistol points naturally. Pointing the pistol will be as natural and easy as pointing your index finger. You can point with your eyes closed and you'll find when you open them that the pistol is pointing at the target.

This is particularly important when the pistol is your backup weapon. You may have the shotgun in one hand, say during reloading, and have to fire the pistol with the other, without using the two-hand grip or the sights.

Can I be sure that a head shot will put down my opponent?

No. First, the brain occupies only the major part of the top half of the head. Second, it depends in part on where in the brain the hit is. The term "head shot" covers a lot of things. Not all areas of the brain are vital areas. Only the medulla controls respiration and heartbeat.

On the other hand, a direct, point-blank shotgun blast in the face is terrifyingly destructive. You will almost always blind the subject and you can usually count on a few pellets cutting the carotid artery on at least one side of the neck and a few others getting to the brain or the spinal cord.

Nothing is sure in this life. The notorious murderer, "Son of Sam," fired at his victims at point-blank range with a .44 caliber revolver and he aimed for the head. Still, he did not get one hundred percent fatalities. In fact, he did not hit all of his victims in the head.

THE SHOTGUN IN COMBAT

The best practice is to be ready to follow up with a quick second shot, unless you have more pressing matters to which you must attend, such as multiple opponents.

I know that physical fitness is very important in other martial arts such as karate and boxing. How important is it in shooting?

It is not quite as important as it is in the other martial arts. It does not take unusual physical strength or coordination to fire a gun accurately. However, this can be a misleading answer even though it is literally true. Practice in shooting is important and the practice must be regular to keep up your shooting skill. That is not what most people consider physical fitness but it is important.

Another thing to consider is that if you expect to defend yourself with a weapon you may well also have to run, jump, and roll in the process. You may have to engage in close combat with your opponent or opponents. You may not be justified or able to shoot and therefore you must be able to handle yourself while using the weapon as a club, or with no weapon at all. That does require some physical stamina, agility, and sometimes just plain strength.

Jogging a few hundred yards each day is the bare minimum that you need to keep in shape. If you can get in a little swimming, or punch a bag once or twice a week that will help. If you have a buddy with whom you can spar, wrestle, or practice whatever hand-to-hand combat you know, better yet. It is unreasonable to expect you to keep in shape like a paratrooper but try to avoid getting fat and flabby.

What gauge shotgun should I get? I don't own one now.

The answer is the same as it is for other guns — the most powerful that you can handle. That usually means a 12 gauge. The 12 is the best choice for several reasons, although other gauges can be very deadly if properly used.

One factor in its favor is power. Nobody can call the 12 gauge anemic.

Another is availability. It is the most common in this country and both the weapons and the ammunition are easy

THE SHOTGUN IN COMBAT

to find. Wherever you go somebody has 12 gauge ammo in stock. This becomes particularly important when you are seeking the anti-personnel loads, such as slugs and double-ought. These are usually readily available only in 12 gauge. The only way to find them in other gauges is to look in the manufacturer's catalog. You won't find many in the stores.

Does having a powerful weapon such as a shotgun make other factors such as tactics less important?

Not really. Even an atom bomb can be used ineptly. Tactics and originality are always important. For example, if you are outnumbered your position will be much better if you can capture one of the enemy and use him as a hostage or a shield.

Improvisations such as a bottle of gasoline can by very useful. In a shoot-out, keep thinking if you are allowed the time. Look around you for anything that will enable you to get an advantage over your opponent and be prepared to do the unexpected.

Should I get one of those shotguns made especially for firing rifled slugs? What are the advantages and disadvantages of these?

The type of shotgun made for firing slugs is bored a little smaller than a regular shotgun and has rifle type sights. It is excellent for firing slugs but little else. If you load it with shotshells you may get overpressure, which might damage the gun. In any event, if you want something that will shoot like a rifle you should get a rifle. If you want a shotgun you should get a shotgun. They have different uses. The slug is just an expedient measure for certain applications but it does not make a rifle out of a shotgun and to get a shotgun that is limited to firing slugs is getting the worst of both possible worlds.

Is a shotgun useful in recapturing an airplane from skyjackers?

Yes. It is a neglected weapon for this application because the military feel more at home with submachine guns and

THE SHOTGUN IN COMBAT

grenades! However, the fact remains that the shotgun is a far more controlable weapon that either a grenade or submachine gun. You do not have the indiscriminate spraying that is so common with those two weapons and, as the patterning tests show, the pattern of shot is tight and very controlable at the ranges found within an aircraft fuselage.

In recapturing an aircraft full of passengers from a band of skyjackers there is inevitably a risk to the innocent. No weapon is certain to harm only the bad guys while sparing the good guys. It is always a calculated risk and when balancing firepower against the risk of killing innocent people it is important to also consider the harm that the skyjackers can do if they are not put down immediately. Time is also important.

For example, a shotgun blast fired in haste that takes out a terrorist armed with a submachine gun and also kills one hostage is better in the long run that a shot that is carefully aimed but only gets the terrorist after he kills a dozen people.

Heavy casualities can be expected. The Israeli raid at Entebbe suggested that this sort of operation can be carried out with almost no innocent lives taken. It is easy to forget that the Israelis sent along a Boeing 707 fitted out as a flying hospital! They expected far heavier casualties than actually occurred. They lucked out and in the afterglow of their success the operation looked far more brilliant than it really was.

With regard to shotguns and weapons in general, how important are stopping power and marksmanship? What is their relative importance?

There is an old saying which I quoted in my other book: "I'd rather be missed by a .45 than hit by a .22!" That says it all.

To give a practical example from real life, the .44 Special is generally considered to be a pretty hefty cartridge. David Berkowitz, the notorious "Son of Sam" used it in firing at people from very close up, sometimes within touching distance. In all cases he was firing at people who could not fire back, as they were unarmed. They were all still targets, not

THE SHOTGUN IN COMBAT

running away. The only adverse condition was that all of the shootings were done at night. The results:

He fired at a total of fifteen people. Three were killed instantly, from head wounds. Two were total misses. Three more died of wounds from three to eighteen hours after they were shot. Of the wounded, two were maimed and the rest made a more or less complete recovery.

That is not impressive performance. People who argue about "stopping power" should keep this in mind. Marksmanship comes first.

It may be belaboring the obvious to point out that if you hit your opponent in the brain with a .22 you will do a lot more to ensure your own survival than if you tear his foot off with a load of double-ought.

What about body armor? What kind should I get which will give me protection against all handgun bullets?

There is no easy answer to that question. Part of the reason is that the question isn't specific enough. Do you mean all handguns you are likely to encounter? All factory loads excluding armor-piercing? All loads including wildcats? Including the Remington XP-100, which although classified as a pistol is really a cut-down rifle?

We'd better start with the fundamentals. First, the main effort in developing body armor in the twentieth century has been to develop something that would be worn. A "bulletproof vest" that weighs forty pounds is not likely to be worn except by those who momentarily expect to be fired upon, such as members of anti-sniper teams. Armor can be designed to resist penetration of even a .30-'06 but it would be too heavy for a policemen, for example, to wear constantly during an eight hour shift. It would be left behind in his locker.

The current crop of vests are mostly made of bullet-resistant synthetic fiber. Note the words, "bullet-resistant." There is no vest made that is one hundred per-cent bulletproof. You can have one that will stop anything up to a .357 and some clown will pierce it with a .44. However, these vests are light, three pounds or so, and not too hot to wear. You will not be deterred from wearing one by the prospect

THE SHOTGUN IN COMBAT

of hours of intense discomfort unless you live in a very hot climate.

Now which one should you buy? The answer is easy. What gun is your next assailant going to use? Go from there. If you don't know, (surprise, surprise) go for something that you can and will wear constantly. One reputable manufacturer is:

      Second Chance Body Armor
      Box 578
      Central Lake, Michigan 49622

He'll even send you a sample of his ballistic cloth to try out. Then you can judge for yourself what its resistance to penetration is. Be prepared for a shock. Some nine millimeter ammo will go through it like a knife through butter. Also, it is not a defense against a knife. A knife, moving more slowly than a bullet, will slash through. It has to do with speed of impact, much like slipping your hand into a pool of water or slapping it down hard. When you slap your hand down hard, the water feels like concrete.

You stated that a shotgun can be very useful in recapturing an aircraft from a hijacker. Can you elaborate on this and suggest some specific tactics?

Yes, I can give you some good do's and don'ts. Remember that tactics are more important than firepower and that intelligent planning can eliminate the need for a protracted shootout.

    1. Control the area surrounding the plane. This means that all people in that area must be authorized personnel and not sightseers, members of the press, or perhaps accomplices of the hijackers. Keep the area sealed off.

    2. Control the press and the electronic media. Do not let them wander indiscriminately around the area, reporting what they see over the air. The hijackers can hear news broadcasts too. Select an area to be reserved for the use of the press and keep them there. Assign an officer to brief the press on the situation as it develops. Do not disclose specific plans and tactics.

THE SHOTGUN IN COMBAT

3. Do not disclose the fact that there are any specially trained anti-terrorist troops in the area. Keep the assault force concealed.

4. Keep the aircraft under observation at all times. This means monitoring the radio as well as visual observation.

5. Try to talk with the terrorists on board. Establish communication with them, as this can be exploited for your purposes later.

6. Your main effort in the negotiations should be to get some of the passengers and crew released. Try to work some sort of a trade — so many passengers in exchange for fuel, or money, etc. This has two purposes; reducing the number of lives in danger and getting you some witnesses to the conditions on board the aircraft. Any people released by the hijackers should be immediately interviewed to find out such pertinent information as:

  a. The number of terrorists on board.
  b. Their weapons. Do they have a bomb too? Who controls it?
  c. The identities of the terrorists, if possible.
  d. The identity of their leader, if any.
  e. Their location inside the aircraft.
  f. The general layout of the situation. Have the passengers been herded into one specific area? Are the terrorists guarding them in shifts? Have they made any threats to the passengers? Have they disclosed their plans to the passengers? What is the apparent mental state of the terrorists? Do they seem reasonable? Frightened? Are the terrorists located in one particular area of the aircraft?

Warn the released people not to talk with the press after their interviews with your officers. Emphasize that disclosure of information could harm the others on the plane.

7. After it is all over, warn the rescued passengers and crew not to discuss specific details of the operation with the

THE SHOTGUN IN COMBAT

media. Such information would be useful to future hijackers. For example, they would never release any hostages if they were aware that they would carry useful information to the anti-terrorist troops.

8. Try to keep some of the terrorists talking, particularly just before the assault. That way you heighten the surprise and also can determine where they are, since you know where the radio is aboard the aircraft.

9. Early in the proceedings obtain plans of the type of aircraft involved. Study them to plan the assault.

10. Have your troops rehearse the assault on a duplicate of the aircraft involved. Usually there is another plane or two of the same type and model at the airport. If not, have one flown in immediately. This is particularly important if the officers under your command are a scratch force, i.e.; Sheriff's deputies, city police, etc. They will not be familiar with the aircraft. If, on the other hand, you command a special anti-terrorist force, they will probably have rehearsed various contingency plans aboard different types of aircraft during training.

AVOID THESE MISTAKES:

1. Never bluff. If they call you you'll have a disaster on your hands.

2. Never threaten. Threats heighten the tension and make it harder to persuade the terrorists to give up, if that is what you are trying to do. Also, threats may provoke the terrorists to kill a few passengers as a response.

3. Do not post your covering or assault troops where they can be seen, particularly by those aboard the aircraft.

4. Don't try anything stupid, such as sending out police or soldiers disguised as ground crew, ambulance drivers, etc. The terrorists will be watching anyone who approaches very closely and will be suspicious of such tactics.

5. Don't fail to keep the troops on alert constantly. You may decide to order an assault on a moment's notice if the

THE SHOTGUN IN COMBAT

situation suddenly worsens, even though you might have previously decided to wait for the cover of night.

6. Don't disclose details of the operation after it is over. Warn your troops against the human and natural tendency to boast of one's successes. That would be just helping future hijackers.